SHAKESPEARE'S
AUDIENCE

SHAKESPEARE'S AUDIENCE

ᏬᎸ

By Alfred Harbage

NEW YORK

COLUMBIA UNIVERSITY PRESS

COPYRIGHT © 1941 COLUMBIA UNIVERSITY PRESS, NEW YORK

First printing 1941
Second printing 1958

Published in Great Britain, Canada, India, and Pakistan
by the Oxford University Press
London, Toronto, Bombay, and Karachi

MANUFACTURED IN THE UNITED STATES OF AMERICA

To
Joseph Quincy Adams

PREFACE

IN THE FOLLOWING PAGES I have collected and tried to interpret justly the evidence on the size, social composition, behavior, and the aesthetic and intellectual capacity of Shakespeare's audience. I have been as objective as it is possible for me to be, realizing that in a reconstruction from fragmentary materials the greatest hazard to the truth lies in the bias of the workman. My desire to avoid distortion explains the infrequency with which I have quoted the plays of Shakespeare himself: they are stimulating texts, and I feared that in a sermon upon men and manners based thereon I might only amaze myself with my own fertility. The plays, by the way, depict audiences—witty and gracious, credulous and passionate, brusque and preoccupied, as the case may be—and, since audiences may be any of these things, it is tempting to derive our conception of Shakespeare's from one he depicts. But Shakespeare's plays were performed in an actual London, not in a dramatically ideal palace of Theseus, forum of Rome, or banquet hall of Elsinore.

Only a brief note on method will be necessary. In quoting from Elizabethan works, I have retained the old spelling except in the few cases where I have expanded abbreviations indicated by archaic symbols, and I have retained the old punctuation except the italics. In both footnotes and bibliography, I have given the date of publication for nondramatic works and the date of first production for plays. Play titles are given in modern spelling and all titles in modern capitalization.

I wish to thank for their friendly interest my colleagues in the Department of English of the University of Pennsylvania, especially Matthias Shaaber, whose sharp eye detected many imperfections in my copy. I wish to thank also Oscar James Campbell, who asked me to speak to the English Graduate Union at Columbia University just at the time my materials had been collected and I would welcome a chance to send up a trial balloon. The recollection of the attitude of this group, alert and sincerely concerned about the issues, and of the invigorating response of Professor Campbell himself lent a zest to the subsequent writing of the book. Finally, I wish to acknowledge the efficiency of the staff of the Folger Shakespeare Library in making my visits profitable and the constant helpfulness of its director. He added to past kindnesses by offering to read my manuscript. Since he had performed such a service on two earlier occasions and since there is a limit to the amount of our writing we may ask our friends to read, I refrained from taking advantage of the offer in spite of the loss to my book. My comfort is that none of its defects can be laid at the door of the one to whom it is dedicated.

ALFRED HARBAGE

Stone Harbor, New Jersey
August 13, 1941

CONTENTS

SHAKESPEARE'S
AUDIENCE

I

THE EVIDENCE

WHEN the first performance of *Hamlet* ended, a column of people streamed into Maiden Lane and then dispersed, radially through the fields and thoroughfares of Southwark, eastward to London Bridge, northward along Horseshoe Alley to the fleet of wherries waiting on the Thames. A litter of nutshells and other debris remained in the darkening cavern of the Globe. The years have sifted into dust the Globe and all who gathered there; no scholarly effort nor feat of the imagination can reverse that ancient process. And even if the miracle occurred, if we could mingle with Shakespeare's audience reincarnate, its secret would prove no more penetrable than the secret of audiences now. What occurs within the minds and hearts of some thousand men and women is not casually revealed: an audience—almost any audience—is as difficult to appraise as the human race itself.

Yet, here is a mystery that we cannot leave alone. How much or how little of *Hamlet* was understood and appreciated by those for whom it was written, what they took from the play and what they were meant to take, what part they played in its creation, whether Shakespeare wrote as he did because of the nature of everyday folk, in spite of it, or both—these questions reach to the core of something larger than dramatic art. They touch upon the worth and destiny of our kind: perfect answers would give us the gift of prophecy.

Needless to say, my little essay will not supply the answers. It is intended to present the evidence with which the answers must conform. It assumes, perhaps invalidly, that we must map the limits of our knowledge, that we cannot be right about the soul of Shakespeare's audience if we are wrong about its body, that the number, kind, conduct, and visible response of the spectators are relevant factors, that we need a scaffolding of fact for the building of conjecture. In view of the nature of the evidence, even my limited aims may be ambitious enough. Elizabethan records are fragmentary, opinions more abundant than facts, and the most willing witnesses not the most credible.

Nothing profitable can now be said of Shakespeare's audience unless we clear our minds of preconception. We must take a long draft of the purgative of doubt, especially concerning opinion. The following typical description of theatregoers was written in 1603, that is, between *Hamlet* and *Lear;* it is the dictum of one Henry Crosse, whose eloquence I revere:

Now the common haunters are for the most part, the leaudest persons in the land, apt for pilferie, periurie, forgerie, or any rogories, the very scum, rascallitie, and baggage of the people, thieues, cut-purses, shifters, cousoners; briefly an vncleane generation, and spaune of vipers: must not here be good rule, where is such a broode of Hell-bred creatures? for a Play is like a sincke in a Towne, wherevnto all the filth doth runne: or a byle in the body, that draweth all the ill humours vnto it.[1]

For "periurie" at least, opportunities in a playhouse must have been limited, not to cavil at other heightened effects.

That we know how to discount such testimony now might be taken for granted. But let me quote from the most cautious and clearheaded of modern stage historians:

plays were not only the occasions for frays and riots, but also brought bad characters together, and were suspected of affording secret opportunities for the hatching of sedition. It must be borne in mind that, so far as the external abuses of theatres go, the complaints of their bitterest enemies are fairly well supported by independent evidence. The presence of improper persons in the theatres is amply testified to by the satirists, and by references in the plays themselves. Intrigues and other nefarious transactions were carried on there; and careful mothers, such as Lady Bacon, anxiously entreated their sons to choose more salutary neighbourhoods for their lodgings. Some serious disturbances of the peace of which theatres were the centres will require attention in the next chapter, while law-court and other records preserve the memory of both grave crimes and minor misdemeanours of which they were the scenes. Like the bawdy-houses, they appear to have been at the mercy of the traditional rowdiness of the prentices on Shrove Tuesday.[2]

No one will rashly impugn the great authority of Sir Edmund Chambers. I am not concerned with what, in general, he knows and believes but with what this particular passage seems to express. It lodges us still, I should say,

---

[1] *Vertues Common-Wealth; or, The High-Way to Honour* (1603), signature Q.

[2] Chambers, *Elizabethan Stage*, I, 264–65.

amidst a "broode of Hell-bred creatures." And it gives us the right to inquire whether it is the legitimate outgrowth of the "independent evidence" mentioned in the text and supplied in the footnotes or whether such evidence will not always be forthcoming by which a preconception may be "fairly well supported." [3] Have Crosse and his kindred labored entirely in vain? Would Chambers have composed this passage had not ancient invectives supplied a mould which time has never been able to break?

Audiences leave few traces behind, few means of vindication. Plays leave their texts for the ages to judge. What would we think of the whole corpus of Elizabethan drama, including Shakespeare's contribution, if we lacked the texts and depended upon contemporary evidence? Let us suppose that William Prynne had exercised the influence in heaven which his ardor deserved, and the page of every playbook had miraculously become blank. The modern historian could easily prove that nothing of value had been lost; in fact, he could come to no other reasonable conclusion. On November 3, 1594, a letter from the Lord Mayor of London to the government at Westminster described contemporary drama:

the same, conteining nothing ells but vnchast fables, lascivious divises shifts of cozenage & matters of lyke sort, which ar so framed & represented by them that such as resort to see & hear the same . . . draue the same into example of imitation & not of avoyding the sayed lewd offences.[4]

---

[3] For the type of evidence cited, see p. 93.
[4] "Dramatic Records of the City of London: the Remembrancia," in *Malone Society Collections*, I, Part I, 75.

Tamburlaine and *Doctor Faustus* were revived at the Rose on the acting days nearest in date to the letter.[5] On September 13, 1595, a new Lord Mayor sent a new letter to the government. Plays contained:

nothing but profane fables, Lasciuious matters, cozonning devizes, & other vnseemly & scurrilous behaviours, which ar so sett forthe; as that they move wholy to imitacion & not to the avoyding of those vyces which they represent.[6]

In 1595 *Romeo and Juliet* and *Richard II* had recently been, or were about to be, added to the repertory of The Theatre. On July 28, 1597, a third Lord Mayor sent a third letter to the government. He saw no necessity for improving upon the descriptions by his predecessors. Plays still contained:

nothing but prophane fables, lascivious matters, cozeninge devises, & scurrilus beehaviours, which are so set forth as that they move wholie to imitation & not to auoydinge of those faults & vices which they represent.[7]

Chapman's *Humorous Day's Mirth* and Shakespeare's *Henry IV* are the extant plays nearest in date to the letter.

No need to point the moral: the descriptions do not fit the plays. The testators had made up their minds and formulated a doctrine, and the facts were not permitted to interfere. A form indictment seems to have been kept on hand, and the creative instinct of the copyist confined to

[5] *Henslowe's Diary*, ed. Greg, I, 20.
[6] "Dramatic Records of the City of London: the Remembrancia," in *Malone Society Collections*, I, Part I, 77.
[7] *Ibid.*, pp. 78–79.

the spelling. The stereotype was already old in 1594–97 and generally familiar. The letters charge that plays "draw apprentices and other seruants from their ordinary workes and all sorts of people from the resort vnto sermons and other Christian exercises." In 1592 Henry Chettle humorously attacked ballads as "full of ribaudrie, and all scurrilous vanity, to the prophanation of Gods name, and with-drawing people from christian exercises." [8] On one occasion Ben Jonson himself admitted "a great part" of the charge that plays (his own excepted) contain "nothing but ribaldry, profanation, blasphemy, all licence of offence to God, and man," [9] and in 1606 a special act of Parliament was required to restrain players from speaking jestingly or profanely of those things which are not to be mentioned but with fear and reverence.

So much testimony of the viciousness of plays exists that we begin to doubt the evidence of the surviving texts. Perhaps they are not representative, and only the least offensive plays were permitted to appear in print. Fortunately, we know better. The plays we read are precisely the ones to which the terms of opprobrium attached. A record like the following is invaluable because it supplies, with the verdict, citation of the particular crime:

The matter of the play is scurrilous, impious, blasphemous in severall passages. One passage of it hath such a bitter Taunt against all Godly persons under the name of Puritans, and at Religion it selfe, under the phrase of observing Fasting days, that it may not be omitted, it was almost in the beginning of

---

[8] *Kind-Harts Dreame* (1592), in Ingleby, ed., *Shakspere Allusion-Books*, New Shakspere Society Publications, Ser. IV, No. I, Part I, p. 47.

[9] Dedication, *Volpone* (1607), in Herford and Simpson, eds., *Ben Jonson.*

the Play, and they were some of the Clownes words when he first began to Act, *Well Ile see my Father hang'd before Ile serve his Horse any more, well Ile carry home my bottle of Hay and for once make my Fathers Horse turne Puritan, and observe Fasting dayes, for he gets not a bitt.*

Aided by this illustration, we are able to find passages that are blasphemous in nearly any Elizabethan play. The writer proceeds to tell us that "the modest, and ingenuous reader would blush to read some passages." Actually, the play is the guileless old fable, *Mucedorus,* perhaps the only virtue of which is its complete innocuousness. Never was there more innocent love-making than appears in the last act, yet the floor of the White Hart Inn at Witney caved in before the village audience could be corrupted. The "Lord from heaven" gave "a check to such wanton sports" a little before "the fancyes of the Spectators were to be filled with the love-complements between Mucedorus, and his Amadine." [10] Portentous and circumstantial, the writer is certain that he is documenting a miracle.

Words are shells: we fill them with our own meanings, and what a freight of meaning some words will bear! The commonest designations for plays throughout the career of Shakespeare were "blasphemous," "lascivious," "obscene," but then any oath or religious figure of speech was "blasphemous," any scene of love-making "lascivious," and any allusion to sex "obscene." Thus, in the balcony scene Romeo's first words to Juliet are "blasphemous":

[10] John Rowe, *Tragi-Comaedia. Being a Brief Relation of the Strange, and Wonderfull Hand of God Discovered at Witney* (1653), signatures *ᵛ, ¶¶2. The date of this tract is late, but the old play and the country locale tend to recreate the atmosphere of sixteenth-century London.

> O! speak again, bright angel; for thou art
> As glorious to this night, being o'er my head,
> As is a winged messenger of heaven.

His every speech is "lascivious"—and his final words are "obscene":

> Sleep dwell upon thine eyes, peace in thy breast!
> Would I were sleep and peace, so sweet to rest!

The morality of Elizabethan drama does not need me as a champion, and the Puritans already have a superfluity of challengers. Details in the plays are truly often coarse and ribald, in Shakespeare's and Jonson's no less than in others', but that the drama in general deserves our values of Elizabethan epithets, the texts themselves triumphantly deny. In the absence of the audience, we cannot take very seriously the terms by which it was officially designated—"the base & refuse sort of people or such yoong gentlemen as haue small regard of credit or conscience." [11]

I shall not labor the point, but the plays would fare no better on aesthetic than on moral grounds were we to judge them in the absence of the texts. The critical silence concerning the popular drama, the lack of prestige attached to dramatic authorship, the flocking of the common people to

[11] The Lord Mayor's letter of November 3, 1594. See "Dramatic Records of the City of London: the Remembrancia," in *Malone Society Collections*, I, Part I, 75. The jig was a particular object of attack and may have deserved it, but in the absence of a representative number of English, not German, texts, I regard the fact that the jig was more than a harmless music-hall "turn" as yet unproved. We may read between the lines in the following passage (Baskervill, *Elizabethan Jig*, p. 136): "In the English pieces taken alone, however, neither bawdy nor clownage plays the part that one might expect from attacks on the jig. . . . Presumably the type of jig that called forth such indignant protest from the better element has not managed to survive in English." Quite aside from what jigs were like, we may notice that if few texts had survived, the passage might have been written about plays.

the theatres—such things would demonstrate that stage plays stood near in the artistic scale to broadside ballads. Commercial evidence of the fact is furnished by the price of playbooks—sixpence—whereas "Literature" in the same bulk cost a shilling.[12] Shakespeare obviously had elected to write not for all time but for the moment. His narrative poems were singled out for praise long after he had given himself over wholly to the theatre. The transitory value of his plays was established by legal process in 1601, when the players deposed after the Essex Rebellion that only a bribe had induced them to revive *Richard II*, which, six years after it was written, was "so old & so long out of vse as that they shold have small or no Company at yt." [13] Isolated defenses of the drama like those by Meres and Harington (both obviously eccentric) would little affect our decision. There are, by the way, isolated defenses of the audience.

Attacks upon plays as such may be regarded as little more than skirmishes in the larger campaign against audiences. Actually, it was the audience that bore the brunt of contemporary hatred, and like most hatreds this one had its basis in fear. The fear was less for the spiritual welfare of the spectators than for the physical comfort and security of those who wished to disperse them. Puritanism, as it suggests a preoccupation with religious and ethical doctrine, explains in only the most meager degree why the death of playhouse audiences—"the great beast . . . the monster of many heads"—seemed, to so many, so infinitely desirable.

The theatre was a democratic institution in an intensely undemocratic age. Nashe wrote:

[12] Plant, *English Book Trade*, p. 220.
[13] The examination of Augustine Phillips, quoted in Chambers, *William Shakespeare*, II, 325.

In London, the ritch disdayne the poore. The Courtier the Cittizen. The Cittizen the Countriman. One Occupation disdayneth another. The Merchant the Retayler. The Retayler the Craftsman. The better sort of Craftsman the baser. The Shoomaker the Cobler. The Cobler the Carman. One nyce Dame disdaynes her next neighbour shoulde haue that furniture to her house, or dainty dishe or deuise, which she wants. Shee will not goe to Church, because shee disdaines to mixe herselfe with base company, and cannot haue her close Pue by herselfe. She disdaines to weare that euery one weares, or heare that Preacher which euery one heares.[14]

The passage occurs in a jeremiad against the sins of the city and must be taken with reservations; yet it is true that the population of London was split into many class-conscious and often mutually antagonistic groups. In the theatres, the rights and privileges of class melted before the magical process of dropping pennies in a box. Distinctions in admission prices and locations were crude compared with finer distinctions of class; thus, in the pit, the cobbler could look at the carman and realize that he was associating with riffraff. Earning an honest living did not establish a presumption of decency. Royal proclamations stigmatized "the popular sort of base condition . . . seruants to artificers . . . such as are of base Manual occupations, and some others wandring by the name of Souldiers returned from the warres." [15] What could be said of a place where such might freely come?

It was because of the democracy of the audience, because "Maisters of this Worshipful Companie and theire deare ffriends coulde not have entertaynmente and convenyente

[14] *Christs Teares over Ierusalem* (1593), in McKerrow, ed., *Works*, II, 135.
[15] *The Queenes Maiesties Proclamation for Staying of All Vnlawfull Assemblies in and about the Citie of London*, July 4, 1595.

place as they oughte to have had" that plays were dispensed with at Merchant Taylors Hall:

Whereas at our Comon Playes and such lyke Exercises whiche be comonly exposed to be seene for money, everye lewd persone thinketh himselfe (for his penny) worthye of the chiefe and most comodious place withoute respecte of any other, either for age or estimacion in the comon weale, whiche bringeth the youthe to such an impudente famyliaritie with theire betters that often tymes greite contempte of Maisters, Parents, and Magistrats followeth thereof.[16]

Thomas Dekker, for all that "Honest labour bears a lovely face," shares the worshipful point of view:

Sithence then the place [the theatre] is so free in entertainment, allowing a stoole as well to the Farmers sonne as to your Templer: that your Stinckard has the selfe-same libertie to be there in his Tobacco-Fumes, which your sweet Courtier hath: and that your Car-man and Tinker claime as strong a voice in their suffrage, and sit to giue iudgement on the plaies life and death, as well as the prowdest Momus among the tribe of Critick.[17]

When Dekker conceived his violent animus against the players, who had fed upon the honey of his wit, the social promiscuousness of their audience became the sharpest arrow in his quiver. The players would "basely prostitute themselves to the pleasures" [18] of plebeians; they were "glad to play three houres for two pence to the basest stinkard in London." [19] The players were peculiarly sensitive to the charge: they, like most of the playwrights, accepted honest labor at the current evaluation and with contemptuous al-

[16] Clode, ed., *Memorials of the Guild of Merchant Taylors*, I, 578.
[17] *Guls Horne-Booke* (1609), in Grosart, ed., *Non-Dramatic Works*, II, 247.
[18] Dekker, *Dead Tearme* (1608), in *ibid.*, IV, 55.
[19] Dekker, *Rauens Almanacke* (1609), in *ibid.*, IV, 194.

lusions to "groundlings" gave a cue which less fastidious times and places have shown an uncritical readiness to follow.

A workingman taking his ease in a theatre was an anomaly. The function of workingmen was to work. A reiterated charge by the civic fathers was that the theatres drew "apprentices and other seruants from their ordinary workes." [20] At Coventry, in 1615, it was obvious that strolling players could not be suffered to perform, with the resultant "drawing of the artificers and common people from their labour." [21] Moral and religious agitation against plays showed less vitality than this; during the Restoration period we hear the old complaint: performances at Norwich "divert the meaner sort of people from their labour in the manufactories, whereby occasioning a vain expense of time and money." [22]

Thus, we see established order about to disintegrate; at any moment the process might be horribly accelerated. Elizabethans had a very real fear of the potentialities of a crowd —any crowd. They were less used to crowds than we are, less adept at policing them, and evidently quite conscious of the degree to which privilege rested more upon precedent than upon any physical power to preserve it. Audiences seemed perfect places for "contrivers of treason and other idele and daungerous persons to meet together." [23] As late as 1619 at Blackfriars, when a fair proportion of the audience was drawing up to the theatre in coaches, the old

[20] July 28, 1597. See "Dramatic Records of the City of London: the Remembrancia," in *Malone Society Collections*, I, Part I, 80.

[21] Chambers, *Elizabethan Stage*, I, 338, note 3.

[22] Rosenfeld, *Strolling Players and Drama in the Provinces*, p. 36.

[23] July 28, 1597. See "Dramatic Records of the City of London: the Remembrancia," in *Malone Society Collections*, I, Part I, 80.

fear persisted: "and what further danger may bee occacioned by the broyles plotts or practises of such an vnrulie multitude of people yf they should gett head, your wisdomes cann conceave." [24] Note the hushed solemnity of the tones. History was ransacked for instances:

For what more fitter occasion to summon all the discontented people together, then Playes? to attempt some execrable actions, commotions, mutinies, rebellions, as it hapned at Windham in Norff. in the time of Ed. the 6 where at a Stage Play (according to a drunken custome there vsed) the horrible rebellion of Ket and his complices, by a watch-word giuen, brake out, to the trouble of the whole kingdome.[25]

To what extent, if at all, the playhouse audiences justified this fear I shall discuss in connection with their behavior in general. We can all agree that crowds in the theatres were inappropriate during the Elizabethan Sabbath and at times of pestilence, but here regulation was soon established without abating one whit the antagonism to audiences.

Perhaps the sharpest thorn in the side of the Lord Mayor and aldermen, and even of the preachers at Paul's Cross, was an economic thorn. It was possible for audiences to make players rich—an unheard-of privilege for such mushroom growths:

We are cammaunded by God to abide in the same calling wheirein we were called, which is our ordinary vocation in a commonweale. . . . So in a commonweale, if priuat men be suffered to forsake theire calling because they desire to walke gentleman like in sattine & veluet, with a buckler at theire

---

[24] *Ibid.*, p. 92.
[25] Crosse, *Vertues Common-Wealth; or, The High-Way to Honour* (1603), signature Q1.

heeles, proportion is so broken, vnitie dissolued, harmony con-
founded, that the whole body must be dismembred.[26]

And as players grew rich, deserving merchants might be
retarded in that natural fulfillment of their own destinies.
In a sense, the theatre was a parasitic industry. It retailed
"wit," and "wit" was not imported or wholesaled by any
of the twelve honorable companies which controlled the
city. Dropping daily into the gatherers' boxes were thousands
of pennies that otherwise might have passed across London
counters:

As for the hindrance of Trades and Traders of the Citie by
them, that is an Article foysted in by the Vintners, Alewiues,
and Victuallers, who surmise, if there were no Playes, they
should haue all the companie that resort to them, lye bowzing
and beere-bathing in their houses every after-noone.[27]

Nashe was a shrewd champion of the drama. So, too, was
Henry Chettle, who repeats Nashe's point and then makes
another which might not occur to us—that the theatres
caused a diversion of pedestrian traffic not beneficial to
certain shopping districts:

But I haue more to say than this; Is it not a greate shame,
that the houses of retaylers neare the Townes end, should be
by their continuance impouerished: Alas good hearts, they pay
great rentes; and pittie it is but they be prouided for. While
Playes are vsde, halfe the day is by most youthes that haue
libertie spent vppon them, or at least the greatest company
drawne to the places where they frequent. If they were sup-
prest, the flocke of yoong people would bee equally parted. But

---

[26] Gosson, *Playes Confuted in Fiue Actions* (1582), in Hazlitt, ed.,
English Drama and Stage, p. 216.
[27] Nashe, *Pierce Penilesse, His Supplication to the Divell* (1592), in
McKerrow, ed., *Works*, I, 214.

now the greatest trade is brought into one street. Is it not as faire a way to Myle-end by White-chappell, as by Shorditch to Hackney? the Sunne shineth as clearly in the one place, as in the other.[28]

How odd that the letters from the Lord Mayors to the Privy Council are silent on these matters. It is significant that the occupational group wholeheartedly in favor of plays was the watermen, who drew much of their income from ferrying the spectators across the Thames.

Behind much of the clamor against the theatres was simple distaste for competition. Larger and larger throngs were following the pied piper. The practice of archery was declining, lamented the Lord Mayor. Voices were even raised on behalf of the "game of beare baytinge." The records of the Privy Council of 1591 preserve the arresting minute that Sundays be reserved for the preachers, Thursdays for the bears. The discomfort of the preacher was acute. Without questioning for one moment his sincerity, we must recognize that he was a human being and fancied himself somewhat as a spellbinder. Could he speak temperately of the sweet song of the siren? His parishioners listened avidly to plays "when as at a Lecture and holy exercise, all the sences are mortified and possest with drowsinesse." [29] Comments on the unfair standards of popular appeal set up in the theatres are sometimes touchingly plaintive.

Most of the testimony on the nature of Shakespeare's audience expresses a social attitude or comes from disappointed poets, disgruntled preachers, wary politicians, or spokesmen

[28] *Kind-Harts Dreame* (1592), in Ingleby, ed., *Shakspere Allusion-Books*, New Shakspere Society Publications, Ser. IV, No. I, Part I, pp. 63–64.

[29] Crosse, *Vertues Common-Wealth; or, The High-Way to Honour* (1603), signature Q2.

for threatened commercial interests. That such is true of the direct testimony is generally recognized, although sometimes unconsciously disregarded. That such is also true of the indirect testimony is not so generally recognized. Many of the facts, the "independent evidence" upon which the audience is convicted of "both grave crimes and minor misdemeanours," have been selected for us, have been preserved, by these same agencies. We cannot expect much of the evidence to be favorable. Certainly we cannot expect it to be more favorable than contemporary evidence on the nature of the plays, which because of, and only because of, the survival of the texts we now practically ignore.

Yet we dare not ignore the unfriendly witnesses on the nature of the audience. Often they are the only witnesses we have. Their charges, moreover, could not have been wholly unfounded: Elizabethan playgoers were not the refined, sedentary, intellectual, and middle-class persons who patronize "legitimate" drama today. Many of them must have been of the earth earthy, asserting themselves in censurable ways. But we are not looking for nice people, as we are not dealing with nice plays. We wish to know what Shakespeare's audience was like. So long as we remember that the points of view of our witnesses are not necessarily our own and that the social and satirical and even moral overtones in their voices no longer concern us, we should listen attentively to every word. Many voices will be heard in the following pages. Some passages are a reticulation of contemporary utterances. Others bristle with ugly statistics. I beg pardon for all and submit a warning: it will baffle us still—that stream of men and women which melted long ago into the lengthening shadows of Southwark.

II

HOW MANY PEOPLE?

IN SHAKESPEARE's own day playhouse audiences were described in terms of "multitudes" and "swarms." The spectator was apt to be "pasted" to the jacket of his neighbor. The churches stood empty, while the theatres were "pestered." In busy seasons "people from all corners of the land" assembled at the plays "in heapes," [1] and "the penny patrons were so glewed together in crowdes . . . that when they came foorth, their faces lookt as if they had been per boylde." [2] But how big is a crowd? No Elizabethan in his whole life saw so many people at one time as will casually assemble in a modern stadium. Not always were there crowds at the theatres regardless of how the term was conceived. Audiences grew thin. Weak companies "broke," and strong companies, though detesting the road, had to leave London and "trauell on the hoofe." [3] The size, at least the average

[1] Dekker, *Dead Tearme* (1608), in Grosart, ed., *Non-Dramatic Works*, IV, 22.
[2] Dekker, *Seuen Deadly Sinnes of London* (1606), in *ibid.*, II, 52–53.
[3] Dekker, *Rauens Almanacke* (1609), in *ibid.*, IV, 196.

size, of the Elizabethan audience remains something for us to find out.

T. W. Baldwin estimates the average daily attendance at the Rose as 453 and at the Globe as 567. The average daily attendance at all theatres between 1599 and 1608 he estimates as between 1,400 and 2,000. For the same period in which Baldwin puts the maximum daily attendance at 2,000, the late Ashley H. Thorndike puts the minimum at 5,000. It would not be surprising if the truth lies somewhere between these extremes, the lowest and highest estimates vouchsafed by close students of the period. Both of them have built upon a false premise, or so I believe, but the delightful process of refutation is limited in appeal and must be relegated to an appendix.[4]

No acceptably scientific estimate of the average size of the Elizabethan audience can be made. Adding together the probable capacity of all theatres operating at once might give us the probable size of the London audience on some banner occasion, a holiday in springtime, but the figure would have little to do with average attendance. A better approach seems to beckon in the theatrical receipts preserved in the records of various companies at various periods. Figures are plentiful, but they prove tantalizingly evasive. When we have receipts for individual sections of a theatre, we lack the receipts for the whole; or when we have the receipts for the whole, we lack the receipts for individual sections. When we know what a housekeeper's share was worth, or an actor's share, we are in doubt about the total number of shares, or deductions for expenses, or prices of admission. The surviving figures simply fail to coöperate.

[4] See Appendix A, pp. 171–73.

What follows is a series of computations culminating in a guess. My only claim is that it is the most thoughtful guess thus far made. The contributory facts have to do with theatre capacities, admission prices, and receipts in a period when the uncertainties are fewest. When assumptions are made, they are clearly indicated. None of the facts are irrelevant, and none of the reasoning is circular. Such guarantees, I believe, are due anyone invited into a realm made dismal by arithmetic.

In 1596 Johannes de Witt, a visitor from Utrecht, described the London theatres and sketched the interior of the Swan. Below are the portions of the description relevant at the moment:

There are four amphitheatres in London of notable beauty. . . . The two more magnificent of these are situated to the southward beyond the Thames, and from the signs suspended before them are called the Rose and the Swan. The two others are outside the city toward the north. . . . There is also a fifth, but of dissimilar structure, devoted to the baiting of beasts. . . . Of all the theatres, however, the largest and the most magnificent is that one of which the sign is a swan, called in the vernacular the Swan Theatre; for it accommodates in its seats three thousand persons.[5]

We are told here, what is otherwise known, that the four London theatres in 1596 are the two to the north (The Theatre and the Curtain) and the two on the Bankside (the Rose and the Swan). Newington Butts has fallen into disuse, but there is a Bear Garden—"of dissimilar structure." By implication, the four theatres are of similar structure,

---

[5] Translated from Arend van Buchell's transcription of De Witt's description, in Adams, *Shakespearean Playhouses*, pp. 167–68. For the most recent reprint of the Latin text, see Chambers, *Elizabethan Stage*, II, 361–62.

and that such was the case is borne out by the fact that, later, the Hope was patterned on the Swan, the Globe was built of timbers from The Theatre, and the Fortune was patterned on the Globe. Theatrical architecture was standardized. De Witt has further informed us that the Rose and the Swan are the most magnificent of the theatres (as they were certainly the newest) and that the Swan will accommodate 3,000 persons in its seats. Observe that he says "in its seats" ("tres mille homines in sedilibus"), meaning, if he is read literally, that the capacity of the house was much greater, since seats were available only in the galleries.

De Witt's figure, even though often mistakenly read as the total capacity of the Swan, has met with determined incredulity; [6] yet 3,000 is his figure, and there is a total absence of contradictory evidence. That 3,000 is a large number, that London was not a vast city, that modern theatres are smaller, is true but immaterial. W. W. Greg's statement that "it is exceedingly difficult to imagine how even the Fortune can have accommodated more than 500 in the galleries" [7] is vulnerable either as an interpretation of the facts or as an effort of the imagination.

The Fortune is the one Elizabethan theatre of which we have the exact dimensions, and knowledge of its capacity and distribution of space will prove of use. The building contract of January 8, 1600,[8] and an exercise of elementary arithmetic reveal that there were 1,842.5 square feet of

[6] Chambers, *Elizabethan Stage*, II, 526, although he believes 3,000 "merely the exaggerated round number of a casual visitor," is more inclined to accept the figure than most and cites Fynes Moryson's mention of the theatres as "capable of many thousands."

[7] *Henslowe's Diary*, ed. Greg, II, 134–35, note 1.

[8] *Henslowe Papers*, ed. Greg, pp. 4–7.

space in the yard unoccupied by the stage. All of this space would be available for standing spectators, and, allowing 2.25 square feet of space per person,[9] 818 persons could be accommodated in this section of the house. The galleries contained 7,156.65 square feet of floor space. Not much more than 80 percent of this would be available for seats, the remainder being consumed by staircases, aisles, and railing space. The available 5,725.32 square feet divided by a 3.75 square foot allowance per sitting spectator [10] gives us a 1,526 person capacity for the galleries of the Fortune. Adding our standing room in the yard, we get a 2,344 person capacity for the house—an estimate in which I have considerable confidence, although I realize that the human frame appears to be compressible and wonders might be accomplished by packing.[11]

We have, at this point, at least a working hypothesis of the capacity of Elizabethan playhouses as suggested by the Swan and the Fortune and, as important, a notion of the relative capacities of yard and galleries. We may turn now to the problem of sections within the galleries and of admission charges to these sections and to the yard. Independent and confirmatory reports survive. In the 1596 edi-

[9] This is a block of space 18 inches square, 18 inches for the width of a man and 18 inches not for the depth but for elbowroom.

[10] This is a block of space 18 inches wide (the width of an ordinary straight chair) by 30 inches deep (the distance from the back of the chair to the occupant's toes). Having made my allotment, I took a tape measure into our football stadium and found that I had been generous. The seats in the Elizabethan galleries probably consisted of rising tiers of benches. The height of the galleries permitted this arrangement ? the Fortune and would otherwise have been excessive.

[11] Corbin, "Shakespeare and the Plastic Stage," *Atlantic Monthly*, XCVII (1906), 372, allows for spectators on the stage and in the tiring-house gallery and makes an estimate, by computing the total length of benches, of 2,138 persons, or 2,558 by packing the house.

tion of William Lambarde's *Perambulation of Kent* is inserted the following:

no more than such as goe to Parisgardein, the Bell Sauage, or Theatre, to beholde Beare baiting, Enterludes, or Fence play, can account of any pleasant spectacle, unlesse they first pay one pennie at the gate, another at the entrie of the Scaffolde, and the third for a quiet standing.[12]

In 1599 Thomas Platter of Basle, as part of his description of the London theatres, wrote:

The playhouses are so constructed that they play on a raised platform, so that everyone has a good view. There are different galleries and places, however, where the seating is better and more comfortable and therefore more expensive. For whoever cares to stand below only pays one English penny, but if he wishes to sit he enters by another door, and pays another penny, while if he desires to sit in the most comfortable seats which are cushioned, where he not only sees everything well, but can also be seen, then he pays yet another English penny at another door.[13]

Numerous casual allusions confirm the scale of prices specified above. A greatly advanced and evidently more variable scale came in with the "private" theatres after 1599, and these in turn modified the price system elsewhere, certainly at the later Globe, but the fact will not distort the present analysis.

Now the question arises what proportion of the galleries was allotted to onepenny places and what proportion to twopenny places.[14] De Witt's testimony again proves helpful.

---

[12] Page 233, quoted in Chambers, *Elizabethan Stage*, II, 359.

[13] *Thomas Platter's Travels in England, 1599*, p. 167.

[14] Failure to consider this point, or rather the assumption that Henslowe's receipts were solely from onepenny seats, invalidates Greg's estimate of the size of audiences at the Rose (*Henslowe's Diary*, II, 134-35, note 1.) The twopenny places were certainly part of the galleries.

The sketch of the interior of the Swan contains the word "orchestra" written under that section of the lowermost gallery nearest the tiring house. The contemporary definition of "orchestra" was "the senators' or noblemen's places in a theatre between the stage and the common seats." [15] The building contract of the Hope, dated August 29, 1613, stipulating that the new house was to be of such "compasse, fforme, widenes, and height as the Plaie house Called the Swan," contains the following specifications: "And shall also make Two Boxes in the lowermost storie fitt and decent for gentlemen to sitt in/ And shall make the pticions betwne the Rommes as they are at the saide Plaie house called the Swan." [16] The section here indicated, "in the lowermost storie," I take to be the section marked "orchestra" in the De Witt sketch—the "Two" meaning one on either side of the stage and the "Boxes" meaning a finished interior of painted walls and plastered ceiling as distinguished from the rough interior of the common galleries. Distortion in the sketch makes the section seem more constricted than it probably was.[17] Since it appears to occupy all that part of the gallery forward of the steps leading up from the yard, and since the best position for the steps to give efficient access to the gallery was midway in the yard, the orchestra would probably run the full depth of the stage on either side, its total area forming about two fifths of the total area of the lower gallery.

[15] From R. Cotgrave, ed., *A Dictionarie of the French and English Tongues* (1611). That De Witt would use the word in the classical sense, as defined by Cotgrave, was pointed out by W. J. Lawrence, *Elizabethan Playhouse and Other Studies*, I, 39.

[16] *Henslowe Papers*, ed. Greg, pp. 19–22.

[17] I am assuming familiarity with the Swan drawing, which is reproduced in nearly all books on the Elizabethan stage.

We could decide on a priori grounds that this would be the choicest part of the Elizabethan playhouse. The spectator is closest to the actors and nearly on a level with them so that he is in the line of vision of the mass of the audience. He "not only sees everything well, but can also be seen." "Lathe lyme and haire" have been lavished upon the ceiling over his head, and, as to the seats, Platter even mentions cushions. His is a position of moderate ostentation. Since he has had to pay a penny at the outer door in addition to the price of his "two-penny room," he has disbursed a total of threepence, but he occupies what Platter calls "the most comfortable place of all." In Dekker's words, "in the moste perspicuous place of the two-penny galleries" he "shall cleerely, and with an open eye, beholde all the partes." [18]

What follows is based upon certain assumptions: first, in absence of specific information about the Rose itself, that the Rose Theatre had seating arrangements approximating those deduced above for the Swan; and, second, that Henslowe's records of receipts from the galleries of the Rose may be interpreted in terms of the three-price admission system specified by Lambarde and Platter and suggested by casual allusions elsewhere, without allowance for the admission charges of sixpence or twelvepence to a "lord's room" which may possibly weight Henslowe's receipts. In view of the nature of the evidence, assumptions must be made, and these I believe are the least hazardous.[19]

[18] *Rauens Almanacke* (1609), in Grosart, ed., *Non-Dramatic Works,* IV, 184.

[19] The Rose certainly had a lord's room: "pd for sellynge of the Rome ouer the tyerhowsse . . . x*s*/ pd for sellinges my lords Rome . . . xiii*s*." (*Henslowe's Diary,* ed. Greg, I, 10.) There is no clue whether the above indicates one room or two; or, if two, whether the first was for spectators or whether the second was in the tirehouse. The lord's room

HOW MANY PEOPLE?

Now to examine Henslowe's record of daily receipts from the Rose. It extends from February 19, 1592, to November 5, 1597, with breaks because of Lent, summer vacations, and various inhibitions to acting. The name of the play performed is given each day, together with a notation when the play is being performed for the first time. That the daily sums entered beside each performance represent half the receipts of the galleries—Henslowe's share as owner of the

---

of the Rose was probably in the tirehouse. Such rooms apparently originated as a section of the upper balcony of the tirehouse, where patrons of the company, or other "Lords," entering through the tirehouse door, paid for their exclusiveness by viewing drama from the rear and missing that part (if such there was) of a play performed on the "inner stage." Sitting on the stage itself was probably an outgrowth of the practice of entering through the tirehouse door. The unsatisfactory position of the lord's room seems to have led to an elaboration of gallery arrangements at the Fortune (1600), possibly at the Globe (1599), and conceivably at the Rose (c.1587). Observe the following specification in the building contract of the Fortune: the galleries shall contain "ffower convenient divisions for gentlemens roomes and other sufficient and convenient divisions for Twoe pennie roomes with necessarie Seates to be placed and sett Aswell in those roomes as througheoute all the rest of the galleries . . . and the gentlemens roomes and Twoe pennie roomes to be seeled with lathe lyme and haire" (*Henslowe Papers*, ed. Greg, pp. 5–6). Clearly, three classes of seats in the galleries are here indicated, and consequently a four-price admission system. But that the lord's room, or any place higher priced than the twopenny rooms, was generally disregarded before 1599, even by literal lords, is indicated by Lambarde and Platter. To me it seems too likely that, at the Rose, the lord's room was inconveniently located in the tirehouse and was unfrequented, or that it was given over to "dead heads," or that its yield was wholly detained by the actors to let it weigh in my calculations. (At the Globe, the rental of the theatre did include the half-receipts of the tirehouse door as well as the half-receipts of the galleries, but at the Globe the most influential actors were also part landlords and stood to lose little if anything by the arrangement.) To counterbalance the possible error introduced by my disregarding possible sixpenny or twelvepenny admissions (which would have been few in any case), there is the fact that Henslowe's actual receipts were greater than the sums he records: there were his fees for gatherers, at least tenpence daily, and there was his habit of not recording odd pennies, meaning an average daily loss to the accounts of twelve halfpence.

Rose—has never been questioned. I shall double all sums, thus giving the whole receipts from the galleries, and shall reduce all sums to pennies, the units of admission charges.

A distinction is observable at once between ordinary performances and opening days. For plays marked "ne" (new), the receipts are uniformly high. For plays not so marked, which for convenience I shall call "old," the receipts are neither uniformly high nor uniformly low. Receipts at old plays range from a low of 72d.[20] to a high of 1,728d.,[21] with all possible gradations between. Receipts at new plays range from a low of 720d.[22] to a high of 1,840d.,[23] also with all possible gradations between. The high receipts at new plays are commonly interpreted to reflect the custom of doubling admission charges at such plays. But observe these figures:

	Low Record	High Record
Old plays	72d.	1,728d.
New plays	720d.	1,840d.

The opinion that the high receipts at new plays are attributable to double admission charges is automatically refuted. If prices in the galleries were doubled, the range of receipts at new plays should rise to 3,456d., that is to double the range of receipts at old plays. But notice that 1,840d. is the limit; in fact, it passes notably the next highest mark. Receipts both at new plays and old plays frequently rise to the neighborhood of 1,700d. and stop. Another indication that the high receipts at new plays are not explainable in

[20] December 9(10), 1594, also December 23(22), 1596. In parentheses are given corrections, usually Greg's, of Henslowe's dates. The years I alter silently to conform to the modern system.

[21] September 30 (October 1), 1594.

[22] December 2(3), 1594, also December 19(18), 1596.

[23] March 3, 1592.

terms of double admission charges is that the average receipts at such plays are not high enough. That the playhouses were crowded at new plays was such common knowledge that "a crowding (as if it had been at a new play)" [24] became with pamphleteers a hackneyed simile. But if the high receipts at new plays as recorded in Henslowe's *Diary* be attributed to double admission charges, we should have to conclude that new plays were somewhat more poorly attended than old ones because the average receipts at new plays were slightly less than double the average receipts at old plays. [25]

The true meaning of the receipts at new plays seems to be as follows. Pressure exerted by the novelty of the play raised the level of gallery receipts, but another kind of pressure prevented these receipts from rising beyond a certain limit. It was the same pressure that prevented receipts from old plays from rising beyond approximately the same limit. This pressure was obviously the capacity of the house.

It might be better to take as "capacity" a 1,700*d*. gallery, but we dare not begin selecting evidence. We have now to view our 1,840*d*. in terms of onepenny and twopenny places. If I am right about the twopenny section (that most "perspicuous" and "comfortable" place of all) occupying about two fifths of the lowest gallery, it occupies about two fif-

---

[24] Dekker, *Newes from Hell* (1606), in Grosart, ed., *Non-Dramatic Works*, II, 118.

[25] Computed over the whole period covered by the *Diary*, the averages are: at new plays, 1,308*d*.; at old plays, 676*d*. The contemporary testimony that higher prices were charged at new plays is susceptible to the following interpretation: the higher charge was made only at the outer door; thus one paid 2*d*. to enter the yard but only the usual rates thereafter. The arrangement would have been sensible. The actors paid for the script and costumes of a new play and merited weighted receipts. The galleries were roomy, and, as the actual receipts show, it was to the landlord's advantage to encourage the actors to perform new plays, for increased attendance meant increased gallery receipts in any case.

teenths of all three galleries, and we are provided with a simple problem in proportions. Approximately 1,408 persons paid 1*d*., and 216 persons paid 2*d*., giving us our total of 1,840*d*. from 1,624 persons.[26] This last figure, representing a capacity gallery at the Rose, is encouraging. From a wholly unrelated body of evidence, my capacity gallery at the Fortune came out to 1,526 persons.[27] The Fortune and the Rose appear to have had gallery capacities nearly alike, and the total capacity of the Rose should be obtainable through an algebraic equation. Thus 1,526 (galleries of Fortune) is to 818 (yard of Fortune) as 1,624 (galleries of Rose) is to *x* (yard of Rose). This works out to 870 persons for the yard, and 2,494 persons for the total capacity, of the Rose.

This maximum attendance of 2,494 persons derives from the maximum gallery receipts of 1,840*d*. The average gallery receipts, calculated to the nearest penny from every performance at the Rose in the year 1595, comes to 778*d*.[28] Another algebraic equation is available: 1,840*d*. (maximum gallery receipts) is to 2,494 persons (maximum attendance) as 778*d*. (average gallery receipts) is to *x* (average attendance). This works out to an average daily attendance at the Rose, in the year 1595, of 1,054 persons.

[26] The equation is $\frac{2}{15} x \times 2 + \frac{13}{15} x \times 1 = 1,840$ with *x* equalling the total number of persons. I have dropped the decimals. The 1,840*d*. was not precisely, of course, the number of pennies collected.

[27] See p. 23. My spectators were comfortably seated with 18 inches of bench room each. More could have been packed in by such crowding as jumped the receipts at the Rose to 1,840*d*.

[28] I have selected the year 1595 because the Rose was open almost continuously and had, in all probability, only a single rival—the Shoreditch house of the Chamberlain's Men. The average receipts for every performance recorded in Henslowe's *Diary* comes to 724*d*., which would give in the equation 981 persons.

A fallacy is observable at this point. The estimate of 1,054 is based on the assumption that the audience distributed itself in the variously priced sections of the house in the same proportions when it was half empty as when it was filled. Common observation warns us that the assumption is probably false. The cheapest places in Elizabethan times, as now, must have exerted a powerful magnetism. At a spectacle the same essential commodity is purveyed to all, and additional expenditure is an investment in prestige and comfort. The lure of the cheap places is combated by showmen by three weapons—scarcity, discomfort, and ignominy. Consider the vast stretch of grandstand and the attenuated bleachers in a modern ball park. A still better illustration is the circus, a universal amusement with an admission system resembling that of the Elizabethan playhouse. At the circus, we may purchase a reserved seat at the entrance, but we rarely do. We pay a general admission charge, only to discover when inside that all seats are reserved except in the brief arcs at the two ends of the tent. A glance instructs us that these are for the brave and hardy and, more often than not, are already crowded. Docilely we negotiate with the inside ticket seller for a place in the more ample and expensive section.

The yard of the Elizabethan playhouse was an uncommonly good place. Only at intervals would sun and rain cooperate with the proprietors in creating discomfort. Of course there was the ignominy of being a penny patron within full view of twopenny and threepenny patrons, and some of the slurs upon "groundlings" in Elizabethan times must be appraised as economic propaganda in the interest of the galleries. An amusing reference to

the shop's foreman, or some such brave spark,
That may judge for his six pence [29]

indicates that, at private playhouses, even a relatively high expenditure would not save one from censure so long as he elected to stay in the cheapest section. But, in spite of all, there must have been many of the young, the poor, the frugal, and the socially robust who would resist all but physical pressure. To leave the yard and enter the galleries, the Elizabethan playgoer had to double his investment. The additional penny dropped in the gatherer's box was a considerable portion of a day's pay—equal, in fact, to what the gatherer himself received for his services during the performance. If we accept 1,054 as the average attendance in the entire house, we must accept 367 as the average attendance in a yard which could accommodate 870. The common pun upon the under*standing* of the penny patrons loses point, for there was room indeed for all to make pads of their coats and sit down, whereupon the position would have been no worse than sitting on the floor of the highest priced section of a modern theatre.

The 1,054, then, is a minimum estimate, for it does not reckon with the probability that part of the gallery patronage at the Elizabethan public theatres resulted from physical pressure, or overflow from the yard. A maximum estimate is obtainable by assuming that the yard was always filled. This gives us an average attendance of 1,557 persons, and it too must be taken with great reservation. It is incredible that the yard was filled to capacity on occasions when Henslowe's receipts reveal only a sprinkling of people in the gal-

[29] Jonson's commendatory verses to Fletcher's *Faithful Shepherdess* (1608).

leries. And on rainy days the galleries might be reasonably well occupied with the yard entirely vacant.[30] I see no way of reconciling the difference between 1,054 and 1,557 except on the principle of repulsion from the two extremes. In the complete absence of data, I shall lean away from the higher extreme and offer 1,250 as the average daily attendance at the Rose in the year 1595. This is my guess, and I have the confidence to believe that it cannot be more than a few hundred off either way. It is to say that the Rose, an Elizabethan theatre of average size, was usually a little more than half filled,[31] its capacity having been designed for attendance at new plays, at the better old plays, and at holiday plays whether good, bad, or indifferent.

If I were the reader instead of the writer of the above excogitation, I would be filled at this moment with confusion and distrust: too many processes for me to follow, too many equations for me to check. Therefore I append, may I be forgiven! the shorter demonstration. Everyone will agree that Henslowe's accounts are a barometer of attendance at the Rose, whatever the difficulties of interpreting them. Everyone will also agree, in view of the many

[30] The theatres were open to the air but not to the skies. The actors were sheltered by their "heavens," and the galleries were roofed, so that plays were performed in all kinds of weather. Only the yard was exposed, and the method of coping with the situation I should surmise, from analogy with the rain-check system at ball parks, to have been as follows: if it was raining before opening time, one reconciled himself to paying at least 2*d.* or staying home; if it began raining after the play had started, the occupants of the yard were permitted to enter the galleries without additional charge.

[31] The distribution would be 563 penny patrons, 595.4 twopenny patrons, and 91.6 threepenny patrons. The value of an average house, then, would be about £8 9*s.* The sum is plausible in view of the fact that £10 was the reward regularly received at this time for a performance at court, and the sum had been calculated upon the assumption that the actors would miss their public performance.

allusions to packed theatres, that the Rose was filled at least on occasion during the year 1595. On Whit-Tuesday of that year an old play was performed, and Henslowe entered in his *Diary* the sum of 792*d*. (a sum approximately duplicated for several other performances of old plays during the year). Let us consider the 792 simply as a reading on a gauge—opposite which is the inscription "Full House." The average sum entered in the *Diary* against performances of old plays in the year 1595 is 366.84*d*. Again let us consider the figure as the reading on a gauge—this time opposite the inscription "Average House." Divide 366.84 by 792 and observe that the average house at the Rose was .463 of the full house. Now what was the full house—the capacity of the Rose? Formerly I let Henslowe's accounts themselves suggest the size of the Rose; at present I rely simply upon analogy. In Fynes Moryson's account, the earlier playhouses were described as "capable of many thousands"; in De Witt's dispassionate description, the Swan would seat 3,000; a modern reckoning from the building specifications illustrates that the Fortune, built with an eye on the Globe, would accommodate 2,344. I maintain that every contemporary indication suggests that the capacity of the Rose was in the neighborhood of 2,500. Multiplying 2,500 by .463 gives us 1,157 persons as the average house at old plays at the Rose in the year 1595. Prices of admission, distribution of spectators, and the like have all been circuited out of the present reckoning; yet 1,157 as the average attendance at *old* plays is still near enough to my estimate of 1,250 at *all* plays with allowance for the probable popularity of the penny places.

We have still to arrive at an estimate of the total number

of playgoers, since we have been dealing thus far only with those attending a single theatre. In the year 1595, the Admiral's Men at the Rose had as their rivals the Chamberlain's Men in Shoreditch, and probably only these. In 1599 the rivalry was greater. "Thus daily," said Platter,[32] "at two in the afternoon, London has two, sometimes three plays running in different places, competing with each other, and those which play best obtain most spectators." In 1595 the company in Shoreditch, the company of Shakespeare and Burbage, was called to play at court three times while the company at the Rose on the Bankside, the company of Chapman and Alleyn, was called only twice.[33] Perhaps we can assume that the Chamberlain's Men were those who played best. I believe we should hesitate before we conclude that they obtained the most spectators. Shakespeare's plays were probably the greatest single popular attraction in the theatrical world of the era; on the other hand, The Theatre and the Curtain were older, probably smaller, and certainly more remote than the Rose. That the Rose had the better location is indicated by the fact that in 1599 the Chamberlain's Men moved to the Bankside. The Admiral's Men,

---

[32] *Thomas Platter's Travels in England, 1599*, p. 167. Platter says "sometimes" there were three plays running the same day, and there are other indications that the boy companies did not perform daily. Using the surviving plays in the period of rivalry between the boys and the men as a gauge, we notice that the number of plays brought out by the boys as compared with the men, even though pieced out with musty antiquities, was scarcely large enough to sustain daily performances at high admission rates. The capacity of the "private" theatres other than Paul's may have been as great as a thousand, although the following is scarcely trustworthy evidence: "if the monster clap his thousand hands" (Nathan Field's commendatory verses to *The Faithful Shepherdess*); "a thousand men in judgment sit" (Beaumont's commendatory verses to *The Faithful Shepherdess*).

[33] Steele, *Plays and Masques at Court*, pp. 108–10.

however much they have been used in modern times for odious comparisons, were a first-rate company, able to match the new theatre of their rivals with a new one of their own a year later. It is safest, I believe, to assume parity and to give the Chamberlain's Men an average audience equal to but not exceeding that of the Admiral's Men in 1595. This gives us a daily average of 2,500 and a weekly average of 15,000 for the total theatrical attendance in London in 1595.

In 1599 there was some burgeoning of theatrical activity with the revival of the boy companies; and in 1602 a third adult company obtained a permanent foothold in London. Five companies, then, were active during the second decade of Shakespeare's theatrical career. The two boy companies, in their smaller theatres and catering to their "select" audiences, probably attracted fewer patrons than any one of the adult companies. Even so, theatrical facilities in London would have doubled, accessibility of playhouses increased, opening days grown more numerous, and stage personalities become more varied. London was growing in size, and the theatres through such stimulation as "wars" made bid for attendance. It does not follow that the size of the average daily audience grew in ratio to the number of companies operating, for more sharers usually mean smaller shares, but the size certainly increased. I introduce at this point the single surviving estimate of the number of playgoers made in Shakespeare's own time. The estimate is well known, but it has labored under the suspicion of being a round number, a mere guess, or an expression of prejudice. In January, 1613, John Taylor petitioned the Privy Council, on behalf of the Watermen's Company, that the actors be forced to resume their activity on the Bankside. Later he wrote an account of his proceedings containing the following passage:

and the players have all (except the Kings men) left their usual residency on the Bankside, and do play in Middlesex far remote from the Thames, so that every day in the week they do draw unto them three or four thousand people, that were used to spend their monies by water.[34]

The King's Men themselves in January, 1613, would have taken up their winter quarters at Blackfriars, although in fairness Taylor concedes that they have not entirely abandoned the Bankside. His figure, however, no doubt covers the entire average daily attendance. Far from being a suspicious article, the "three or four thousand" is, I believe, exactly right. Unlike other numbers, difficult to determine and encouraging wild guesses, the number of playgoers, then though not now, was pretty widely known—by actors, officials, investors in theatrical properties, gatherers, and even by habitual playgoers. Taylor himself, as an intimate of the actors, was in an excellent position to know and would have been foolish to make a misstatement which the playhouse proprietors, who were fighting the petition, and the Master of the Revels, who would have been advising the Privy Council, could immediately refute. Finally, 3,000 to 4,000 in 1613 is precisely what might be deduced from our estimate of 2,500 in 1595. About 2,500 a day or 15,000 a

[34] *The Trve Cavse of the Water-Mens Suit concerning Players*, in Hindley, ed., *Old Book Collector's Miscellany*, II, 6–7. The pamphlet contains what seems to be one obvious overestimate—that between Windsor and Gravesend there are forty thousand watermen and "those that live or are maintained by them" (p. 6). But this is a very different type of figure from that relating to playgoers: by a process familiar among amateur economists the forty thousand estimate might have been increased to include the whole population of London.

[37]

week in 1595, about 3,000 a day or 18,000 a week in 1601, about 3,500 a day or 21,000 a week in 1605—this is my conjecture of average theatrical attendance in Shakespeare's day.[35]

What proportion does this represent of the total population of London? Any answer will be a multiple conjecture because it is now as difficult to come by a knowledge of the number of inhabitants of old London as of the number of playgoers. Yet an answer must be attempted, for the number of playgoers, if known to a man, is of little significance in itself.

One difficulty lies in the indeterminate use of the term "London." With vexing frequency, population figures are volunteered without explanation of which of the four possible areas the figures are supposed to cover: the intramural City; the City with its liberties and outer wards; the City, its liberties and outer wards, and the outparishes included in the bills of mortality; or all these, together with Westminster and Lambeth to the west, Newington Butts to the south, and Stepney and other small communities to the east. Obviously it is the last, the entire "metropolitan area," that concerns the historian of drama, since the same restricted number of theatres served all.

The tendency in recent years has been, I believe, to overestimate, at least in literary studies, the population of this area in Shakespeare's time, because of the influence of a

---

[35] In 1601 four companies were operating, in 1605 the full number of five. Theatrical attendance, I believe, reached its peak and leveled off while London was still rapidly growing, so that Taylor probably gives us an upper limit which had already been reached by 1605. That the audience did not continue to grow is suggested by increased admission charges, stringencies in the affairs of the companies, and more subtly by the changing character of the plays themselves, which were directed more and more to a restricted class.

[38]

well-known essay by Dr. Creighton.[36] He uses, as one must, such vital statistics as are available for the period, and from them estimates 152,478 as the population for 1595 and 224,275 for 1605. To how large an area the first figure applies I am uncertain, but by 1605 the populous out-parishes were within the bills of mortality used by the writer; however, Westminster and the hamlets neighboring London are not embraced in the survey. The difficulty with Dr. Creighton's estimates is that they are computed on the basis of a birth rate of 29 per 1,000 and a death rate fluctuating between 23 and 25 per 1,000, neither of which has any authority other than being "not unusual" in 1891, and both of which are quite incredible for 1595–1605. The death rate in Shakespeare's time was certainly more than 25 per 1,000, or 1 in 40. A sounder estimate is arrived at by F. P. Wilson,[37] whose method is to add 10 percent to the bills of mortality as allowance for possible omissions in the returns and to use a death rate of 1 in 30, with the reservation that it is too low and will provide only an upper limit of population. Applied to the year 1605, when the bills of mortality returned 5,948 nonplague deaths in "greater" London, this method gives us a population of 196,260 as an upper limit as compared with Creighton's population of 224,275.

Obviously, greater refinement depends upon the use of a more accurate death rate. In 1631, a kind of summary census [38] (now generally distrusted) gave 130,163 as the population of London with its liberties and outer wards. For

[36] Creighton, "The Population of Old London," *Blackwood's Magazine*, CXLIX (1891), 477–96.

[37] *The Plague in Shakespeare's London*, pp. 214–15.

[38] Reprinted in Rogers, *History of Agriculture and Prices in England*, VI, 711.

the same year the bills of mortality returned 6,156 nonplague deaths for this area. Without manipulating either figure, since the census returns seem even more likely than the bills of mortality to have contained omissions, we get 1 in 21.1 as the death rate in 1631. The rate may be too high for the portion in question and yet not too high for the whole metropolitan area, since the outparishes (not used in the reckoning) always showed a higher death rate than the rest. Finally, in 1696 Gregory King, the first "political arithmetician" whom modern economists take seriously, gave 1 in 24.1 as the death rate for the entire metropolitan area.[39] I believe that we are safe in assuming that the rate was at least 1 in 24.1 in 1605.

Let us now take the 5,948 nonplague deaths of 1605 as they stand and use our high death rate of 1 in 21.1. This gives us a population of 125,502—a minimum estimate. Then let us take 5,948 deaths, add 10 percent for possible omissions in the bills of mortality, and use our low death rate of 1 in 24.1. This gives us a population of 157,662—a maximum estimate. The compromise figure is 141,582 for the population of London and its outer wards and outparishes in 1605.

There remain to be accounted for the outlying districts

---

[39] "Natural and Political Observations," in Barnett, ed., *Two Tracts by Gregory King*, p. 27. The figure actually reads 1 in 14.1, but that this was owing to a slip in copying may be seen by dividing King's 22,000 deaths into his 530,000 population, which gives us the rate of 1 in 24.1. A study by Jones and Judges, "London Population in the Late Seventeenth Century," *Economic History Review*, VI (1935–36), 45–63, I believe tends to confirm King's death rate. The article provides a burial rate of 1 in 29.6 for the city within the walls (p. 61), and 1 in 22.1 for the outer wards (p. 62), while it hazards no estimate for the more fatal outparishes.

of Westminster, Lambeth, Newington Butts, Savoy, Stepney, Hackney, and Islington. An isolated record of mortality
in these districts in 1603 [40] reveals nonplague deaths at the
rate of 744 a year. On the basis of this record, we should
place the population of these districts at about one sixth that
of the larger area already accounted for. But 1603 was a
plague year, and in such years the number even of those
deaths not attributed to plague was always abnormally high.
A safer estimate is about one eighth, or 17,698 people, about
half of them belonging to Westminster.[41] Adding these to
the 141,582 already obtained gives us 159,280, or, in round
numbers, 160,000 for the population of the entire metropolitan area of London served by the theatres in 1605.

Viewing this figure, 160,000, in relation to the estimate
of 21,000 weekly spectators at the theatres in 1605, we
should say that 13 percent of the population, or 2 persons
in 15, went to the theatres each week, the proportion holding roughly, I believe, for the whole period of Shakespeare's
theatrical career. What then of the oft-used analogy of
theatre attendance in Shakespeare's day and movie attendance in our own? Eighty-five million Americans are said to
go to the movies every week—about 65 percent of our
population, or 10 persons in 15. In the light of this modern

[40] Printed in Wilson, *The Plague in Shakespeare's London*, p. 184.
Since the record is fragmentary, I have calculated the yearly death rate
from the monthly rate and have assumed that the record for Lambeth
covers the same period as that for Westminster and that those for Hackney and Islington the same period as the record for Stepney.

[41] Brett-James, *Growth of Stuart London*, p. 498, believes Westminster's population to have comprised about half the total of the outlying London metropolitan area, but places this total in 1605 at between 20,000 and 30,000. He is, however, influenced by the inflated
estimates for London made by Creighton.

[41]

devotion to drama, the Elizabethan Londoner begins to appear almost apathetic. But I shall say more about this analogy later on.

We cannot, of course, infer that it was the same 13 percent of the population who went to the theatres every week. The actual number of playgoers was greater than this, since many, especially in view of the difficulties to be discussed in a later section, would have been able to attend only at infrequent intervals. Nevertheless, there are indications that the total number of playgoers was strictly limited. One piece of evidence is the drawing power of new plays. The fact that audiences nearly doubled in size on each opening day indicates not only an efficient system of posting and announcement on the part of the actors but habitual playgoing on the part of the spectators. The best reason for selecting a new play to see is that the spectator has seen all the old ones. A large percentage of the audience must actually have gone to the theatres about once a week, alternating between the companies. Some went more often—Fuscus for instance:

> He's like a horse, which, turning round a mill,
> Doth always in the self-same circle tread:
> First, he doth rise at ten; and at eleuen
> He goes to Gyls, where he doth eate till one;
> Then sees a Play till sixe, and sups at seven;
> And after supper, straight to bed is gone;
> And there till ten next day he doth remaine,
> And then he dines, and sees a Comedy
> And then he suppes, and goes to bed againe:
> Thus round he runs without variety.[42]

---

[42] Sir John Davies, "In Fuscum," Epigram No. 39, in Grosart, ed., *Complete Poems*, II, 37–38.

[42]

But for many more, like Goodwife Nell in *The Knight of the Burning Pestle*, going to the play was a rare treat.

Some idea of the total number of playgoers is suggested by the records of individual plays in Henslowe's accounts. An average run consisted of about twelve performances spaced a week or so apart, usually with the first six showing higher than average receipts and the second six lower, the total impression conveyed being of a quickly exhausted clientele. Sometimes it required only a second or third performance to send receipts to below average, whereupon the company realized that it had "laid an egg" and withdrew the play.[43] Other plays were palpable "hits," and these are a better gauge of the aggregate number of London playgoers. *Wise Man of West Chester* was such a hit. Its total yield to the galleries was 26,400*d*. The ratio I have previously worked out of 1,250 admissions to each 778*d*. collected in the galleries gives us 42,416 total admissions to this play. Many of these must have been of spectators seeing the play a number of times. The repeated performance of old favorites, like *Faustus*, is sufficient evidence of the willingness of playgoers to see certain plays more than once.[44] On the other hand, by the time *Wise Man of West Chester* had been performed its thirty-two times over a period of more than two years,[45] and had brought in its 26,400*d*., we can assume that practically everyone who went to the theatre at all had

[43] *Julian the Apostate*, for instance, was played the third (and last) time May 20(21), 1596, with 336*d*. collected in the galleries, against a daily average of 669*d*. for the year.

[44] Samuel Pepys, the first Londoner of whose playgoing habits we have complete information, scarcely had his teeth in a play until he had seen it two or three times.

[45] December 2(3), 1594, to July 18, 1597.

gone to see this play. The total number of playgoers in the London area, then, was probably a good deal under 42,416 persons in the period from 1594 to 1597, although in 1595 about 15,000 were going weekly. As an estimate, I should say that the theatres drew their weekly attendance of 13 percent of London's population in spite of the fact that over two thirds of that population never attended.

The selective nature of the audience is significant and will concern us in the later sections of the present study. So far as I can anticipate criticism, I suspect that my estimate of theatrical attendance will seem too high and my estimate of the population of London too low. My conclusions in these matters are at variance with my own initial "general impressions." However I have followed the traces whither they appeared to lead. If there were indeed fewer playgoers and more Londoners than my analysis would indicate, then my salient point is all the more true—that only a minority of Londoners were habitual playgoers and the majority were not playgoers at all.

Certain habits of theatrical attendance are revealed by Henslowe's receipts without need for speculation. An electrical calculating machine and patience have enabled me to obtain a series of revealing averages, which I present in appended charts. The chart of workdays [46] shows no particular day of the week especially allotted to playgoing. Monday was somewhat better than other days, probably because of the enduring reluctance of mankind to return to work after Sunday. New plays were almost invariably brought out from Tuesday through Friday—not on Monday, a good day in any case, and not on Saturday. Why not on Satur-

[46] See Chart I, Appendix B, p. 174.

day? Was this also a good day in any case, and is our chart misleading in this detail? I am inclined to think that Henslowe paid his gatherers and discharged other small expenses out of receipts on Saturdays and on the last day of the month, thus distorting our attendance chart. So far as the custom had made progress in establishing itself in Elizabethan times, Saturday was the worker's half day. We must remember, of course, that the average worker would have stayed in the yard. But the impression that playgoers generally, including those in the galleries, were taking time off from work is fortified by the averages of holidays.[47] Careful not to waste attraction, the actors never brought out new plays on holidays, when a good audience was already insured. The Reformation has obliterated Corpus Christi Day as an occasion for playgoing. The surprisingly good attendance on Ash Wednesdays may be another manifestation of Protestantism —or perhaps only a sign that Londoners knew the playhouses might soon be closed for the remainder of Lent. Whitsuntide and the Boxing days are the liveliest times of all—and so, in London, they have remained.

The most interesting variations in attendance are seasonal. The period 1594–95, when acting was uninterrupted and competitive conditions stable, provides the best picture.[48] Attendance is good in the summer and early autumn, gradually diminishing as cold weather sets in, then rising to a peak in the pleasant days of spring. In 1595–96 the same trend is observable, except that the expected recovery does not occur in April, May, and June—an indication, perhaps, that the Swan Theatre has been completed in time to open

[47] See Chart II, Appendix B, p. 175.
[48] See Chart III, Appendix B, pp. 176–77.

up after Lent [49] so that the Rose is feeling the knife of competition. The period 1596–97 follows roughly the trend of the preceding periods but on a reduced scale. Again competition from the Swan may be the reason, but another is more probable: the period was one of dearth and cruel poverty in London and all England. The pre-Lenten month of February is good in all three periods. The legal terms, when the town houses of the gentry and the inns and boarding-houses of Westminster were filled, show less influence on attendance than contemporary allusions would lead us to expect. Michaelmas term does little for attendance in November, or Hilary term for January. Easter and Trinity terms come almost side by side in a season naturally benign. Lent has passed, the Easter and Whitsun celebrations give a lift to the mind, and a holiday spirit is abroad in the land.[50] A combination of things accounts for these teeming "Tearm times, when the Two-peny Clients, and Peny Stinkards swarme together to heere the Stagerites." [51] In all three periods either November or December is the poorest month, a reminder that theatres were open to the air and Elizabethans were not impervious. Yet when we realize that Shakespeare's fellows, and their rivals at the Rose, must often have had to sweep from their stages the snow which had sifted under the heavens, that the galleries were dank, the yard mucky underfoot, the distance from home considerable, we must marvel that midwinter kept little more

[49] Some time in 1595 or 1596 has hitherto been the nearest date, supported by evidence, ventured for the completion of the Swan.

[50] Throughout the accounts, holidays, like Sundays on a lesser scale, bring good days in their wake.

[51] Dekker, *Worke for Armourours* (1609), in Grosart, ed., *Non-Dramatic Works*, IV, 96.

than a third of the full springtime audience away from the beloved plays.

Most of the present section of my discussion of Shakespeare's audience has had to do with the rival company. This is an exigency of the case: no landlord of the Chamberlain's Men has left us a diary. Moreover, whatever of purely external fact is discoverable about the audience of his rivals applies with about equal force to the audience of Shakespeare himself. So long as the activities of the Admiral's Men and the Chamberlain's Men were so nearly parallel, we are foolish to ignore analogy and resort to pure surmise. What I wish to do now is to link the preceding discussion specifically with Shakespeare.

In 1601, the probable year of *Hamlet,* a third adult company has not yet succeeded in gaining a permanent foothold in London, but the boy companies, renewed and vigorous, "berattle the common stages" while the playwrights berattle each other. With the average daily attendance at all theatres about 3,000 and with a fair share, especially of the better-paying patrons, going to the boys, Shakespeare's company may have felt the pinch, performing their older plays before audiences of fewer than a thousand

HAMLET.   Do the boys carry it away?
ROSENCRANTZ.   Ay, that they do, my lord; Hercules and his load too.

but they would not have been forced to tour. Shakespeare the actor would have been more affected than Shakespeare the writer: attendance at his own plays would have been little diminished. *Hamlet* itself, on opening day, would have drawn between 2,000 and 3,000 spectators, depending upon the capacity of the Globe, and thereafter, judiciously alternated with older plays, large but gradually dwindling audiences until it too had become an older play. The process would have taken two or three months, by which time the majority of the spectators would be repeaters able to quote considerable passages in the manner of the actors. Launched upon its career as the greatest theatrical attraction of all time, *Hamlet* would never be dropped from the repertory but would always be good for a better than average audience. So with the best of his other works. Coming as they did at the rate of two a year, Shakespeare's plays competed with each other and some might fall into desuetude, but when a play by Shakespeare was selected and billed, whatever its age, the actors would have been surprised to see fewer than 1,000 spectators.

Lest it savor of bardolatry, I must hasten to explain that the foregoing sketch derives from analogy with the careers of successful plays in Henslowe's *Diary*, where stage histories are recorded in shillings and pence. It derives especially from analogy with the stage histories of plays by Marlowe and of one by Shakespeare himself. On March 3, 1592, *Henry VI*, Part I, had its opening at the Rose, and brought in as gallery receipts the all-time record of 1,840*d.* previously noted in the present study. In the following three months, it was performed thirteen additional times. During the first nine of these, the receipts on five different occasions equaled those normally taken on opening days. The four remaining performances show average receipts, the last, June 20, 1592, coming three days before a summer intermission. Before the record resumes, Thomas Nashe's *Pierce Penilesse* was entered in the Stationers' Register,

August 8, 1592. In the pamphlet, Shakespeare's play is thus signalized:

How would it haue ioyed braue Talbot (the terror of the French) to thinke that after he had lyne two hundred yeares in his Tombe, hee should triumphe againe on the Stage, and haue his bones newe embalmed with the teares of ten thousand spectators at least (at seuerall times), who, in the Tragedian that represents his person, imagine they behold him fresh bleeding.[52]

"Ten thousand spectators at least," says Nashe of the first run of this play, and probably nearer 20,000, since the fourteen performances "grossed" in the galleries 14,156d. —a record surpassed by only one other play mentioned in Henslowe's *Diary*.[53] When Strange's Men left the Rose, the *Diary* had no more to say of *Henry VI*, Part I, but more would be needless. Henslowe and Nashe, earliest recorders of a Shakespearean play, agree on its power to draw an audience.

Shakespeare did not lose ground. Sparse as the subsequent records are, they are more abundant for his plays than for those of any contemporary playwright. In 1598, we hear that "Shakespeare among the English is the most excellent in both kinds for the stage"; [54] about 1601, that Hamlet has in it "to please the wiser sort"; [55] about 1603, that "our fellow Shakespeare puts them all downe"; [56] in 1604, that

[52] *Pierce Penilesse, His Supplication to the Divell* (1592), in McKerrow, ed., *Works*, I, 212.
[53] *Wise Man of West Chester*. We can compare the records of the two plays only for the first leg of the race; *Henry VI*, Part I, may have won the second.
[54] Meres, *Palladis Tamia*.
[55] Gabriel Harvey, *Marginalia*, ed., Moore Smith, p. 232.
[56] *The Return from Parnassus*, Part II, Act IV, Scene iii, in Macray, ed., *The Pilgrimage to Parnassus*.

"to come home to the vulgars Element . . . Friendly Shakespeare's Tragedies . . . please all"; [57] in 1609, that "the most displeased with Playes, are pleasd with his Commedies"; [58] and finally, we hear the famous summing up:

I doe not wonder when you offer at
Blacke-Friers, that you suffer: tis the fate
Of richer veines, prime judgements that have far'd
The worse, with this deceased man compar'd.
So have I seene, when Cesar would appeare,
And on the Stage at halfe-sword parley were,
Brutus and Cassius: oh how the Audience,
Were ravish'd, with what wonder they went thence,
When some new day they would not brooke a line,
Of tedious (though well laboured) Catilines;
Sejanus too was irkesome, they priz'de more
Honest Iago, or the jealous Moore.
And though the Fox and subtill Alchimist,
Long intermitted could not quite be mist,
Though these have sham'd all the Ancients, and might raise,
Their Authours merit with a crowne of Bayes.
Yet these sometimes, even at a friend's desire
Acted, have scarce defraied the Seacoale fire
And doore-keepers: when let but Falstaffe come,
Hall, Poines, the rest you scarce shall have a roome
All is so pester'd: let but Beatrice
And Benedicke be seene, loe in a trice
The Cockpit Galleries, Boxes, all are full
To heare Maluolio that crosse garter'd Gull.

---

[57] Anthony Scoloker, *Epistle to Daiphantus; or, The Passions of Love*, in Chambers, *William Shakespeare*, II, 214–15.

[58] Also in 1609, we hear that (*Pimlyco or Runne Red-Cap*, in Chambers, *William Shakespeare*, II, 217):

all the Roomes
Did swarme with Gentiles mix'd with Groomes,
So that I truly thought all These
Came to see *Shore* or *Pericles*.

These lines by Leonard Digges first appeared in print in 1640, prefaced to Shakespeare's *Poems*, but Digges had then been dead for five years and it is virtually certain that they had originally been written as part of his commendation of the Folio of 1623. Since Ben Jonson also contributed verses to the Folio and it was Jonson's audience that Digges used for odious comparison, a tactful excision seems to have been forced upon the publishers.

If we know anything about the Elizabethan stage, we know that Shakespeare was its most popular writer. The size of the average audience, then, to which I have devoted so much space, was the size of Shakespeare's audience at its minimum. What it meant to him in the way of stimulus and reward to see his new plays normally acted before two thousand and more spectators and his old plays before a thousand and more spectators may be inferred. One point must be made, and in the present statistical atmosphere it may seem less offensive than elsewhere; in writing two plays a year Shakespeare was operating at maximum commercial efficiency. To keep attendance at a maximum, the market being what it was, his company needed this much from him and no more. In fact his retirement was no catastrophe, and Shakespeare himself may head the long procession of playwrights oppressed by the Shakespearean repertory. There seems no doubt that for whomever else he wrote—and it was certainly not the book trade—Shakespeare wrote for his audience. Play production was as grim a business then as now. Let us take a parting glance at the stage histories in Henslowe's *Diary*. *Julian the Apostate* with three performances was a failure; *Philipo and Hippolito* with twelve, an average success; and *Wise Man of West Chester* with thirty-two, a great hit. Reckoning roughly each performance as worth £8 to the theatre (although those of failures were worth less), the first play brought in £24, the second £96, and the third £256. A play had to be bought, costumed, and rehearsed, all of which consumed time, effort, and money. The difference between £256 and £96 was exhilarating, the difference between £96 and £24 disastrous. The fact that some £24 play might be ordered for court and liked would lighten the catastrophe by only £10. And the court would not like the £24 play anyway. If Shakespeare wrote for the court or for some hypothetical alter ego who perused his manuscripts, how fortunate for him and for us that his audience—so many people—were willing to tolerate so much merit.

III

WHAT KIND OF PEOPLE?

SOME FUTURE AGE may take the satirical portraits which
our journalism has produced—of traveling salesman,
social butterfly, collegiate youth, and the like—and attempt
to recreate our audiences. The results will be peculiar. Audiences never are assemblies of caricatures. We are obviously
in error if we people the Globe with multiples of Davies'
Inns-of-Courtier, Dekker's Gull, Beaumont's Apprentice,
and Fitzgeffrey's Bobadil.[1] Only one alternative is open
to us: we must think of the many thousands of Londoners
and the many factors governing their selection of pastimes
—such factors as purchasing power, available time, religious
scruples, age, sex, and personal tastes. Thus we may obtain
some idea of the several thousand representatives sent forth
from the city to gather about *Hamlet* one weekday afternoon a long time ago.

The theatres, I have estimated, were within walking dis-

[1] The "types" are pleasantly assembled by Byrne, "Shakespeare's Audience," in Shakespeare Association, *A Series of Papers on Shakespeare and
the Theatre*, pp. 186–216.

tance of 160,000 people in 1605, of slightly fewer in 1601. These thousands were divided into various classes. Lamenting in 1616 that the weakness of men and the "pride of women" drew many people from the country "because the new fashion is to bee had no where but in London," King James made a summary pronouncement: "And now out of my owne mouth I declare vnto you . . . that the Courtiers, Citizens, and Lawyers, and those that belong vnto them, and others as haue Pleas in Terme time, are onely necessary persons to remaine about this Citie; others must get them into the Countrey." [2] Had the order been obeyed, the term "Citizens" read literally, the London area would have been largely depopulated. A more useful idea of the major divisions of urban population is provided by a muster roll of 1608,[3] classifying the men between twenty and sixty years of age in the towns of Gloucester, Tewkesbury, and Cirencester. The following is a simplified analysis showing the percentage of each classification:

Gentry, professional men, and officials	6.3
Dealers and retailers	19.3
Craftsmen	52.0
Laborers, carriers, etc.	(c)15.0
Servants and miscellaneous	(c)7.4

The classification is only suggestive, even as applied to the towns of Gloucester county, and has no authority for London; nevertheless, it gives us a starting point. In the London area, the presence of the court with all its administrative offices—particularly the law courts with their appendages,

[2] "A Speach in the Starre-Chamber," June 20, in *Political Works*, ed. McIlwain, p. 344.

[3] Tawney and Tawney, "An Occupational Census of the Seventeenth Century," *Economic History Review*, V (1934–35), 36.

the Inns of Court and Chancery—and the standing of the city in the world of fashion would have raised the proportion of "Gentry, professional men, and officials" perhaps to as high as 10 percent. At the other end of the scale there is a category wholly unaccounted for in the muster roll—what Gregory King was later to call "Transitory People"—cashiered soldiers and seamen ashore, as well as vagrants, paupers, thieves, and peddlers. Shakespeare's London probably succeeded in submerging more than the traditional tenth.

But when all adjustments are made, the group remaining by all odds the largest, although not so large as 52 percent of the whole, will be the "Craftsmen"—the carpenters, masons, bookbinders, and button makers, with their helpers, the whole contingent of artisans, or "handicraft men," and those who were dependent upon them. It is with this group that we had better begin.

In 1601 the average weekly wage for artisans in England, master workmen and helpers together, was about 5s. 3½d. per man; a bricklayer or mason received 1s. a day, his helper 10d.[4] Artisans in London, however, were paid above the average. Between 1593 and 1602 the masons working on London Bridge received between 14d. and 16d. a day [5] as compared with the national average of 12d. Since the building crafts paid somewhat more poorly than the newer industries,[6] we may take the higher figure, or 16d., as representing the average daily wage of master workmen in London. This is 33⅓ percent more than the national aver-

---

[4] Rogers, *History of Agriculture and Prices in England*, V, 664–65, 826.

[5] Knoop and Jones, *Mediaeval Mason*, p. 236.

[6] Nef, "Prices and Industrial Capitalism in France and England, 1540–1640," *Economic History Review*, VII (1936–37), 164.

age; hence the weekly wage of London workmen generally may be put at 33⅓ percent more than the national average of 5s. 3½d. Exactitude in the matter is scarcely possible, but we shall err by very little, and probably on the side of generosity, if we place the average weekly wage of London workmen at 7s. in the year of *Hamlet*.

Fortunately, my task is not to explain how workmen lived and reared their children. That prices had terribly outdistanced wages by 1601 is common knowledge. For Dekker, despite the breadth of his sympathies, workmen were "Stinkards": herrings and onions, alas, were among the few foods they could afford to buy; bread was an expensive luxury. As we review the cost of other pleasures as compared with that of theatregoing, it will be helpful to keep in mind the earnings of workmen today as a relative gauge. Skilled craftsmen, such as earned 16d. a day in Shakespeare's London, no longer form a large percentage of wage earners; they are now, deservedly, a highly paid aristocracy. The most appropriate figure to use for equation is the average weekly wage of the millions of contemporary industrial workers. In America, in the month of the present investigation, that wage is $25.46 or 98.2 percent of the 1923–25 norm.[7] The norm appears to be $25.93 as the average weekly wage of modern American industrial workers, as compared with the 7s. average weekly wage of workmen in Shakespeare's London. Considered as a proportion of income, each penny spent by a workman then was equivalent to each 31 cents spent by a workman now. The wage earner of that time, therefore, could go to the theatre almost as cheaply as his modern

[7] U.S. Bureau of Labor Statistics, *Monthly Labor Review*, LI (1940), 474.

counterpart can go to the movies. We shall see that he could purchase no other pleasures at modern rates. I am speaking, of course, of commercialized pleasures: fortunately, the Elizabethan could walk into the country and "drink the waters of the crisped spring."

Nashe gives the following alternatives for spending a vacant afternoon in London: "that pleasure they deuide (howe vertuously it skils not) either into gameing, following of harlots, drinking, or seeing a Playe." [8] An earlier pamphleteer lists as "the places of expense" the taverns, the alehouses, The Theatre and Curtain, and Paris Garden.[9] With the following of harlots we need not linger, except to remark that the terms "sixe-penny whoredome" and "six-pennie damnation" [10] give an idea of the minimum rate. Paris Garden was the center of bearbaiting; and bearbaiting, like cockfighting and even bowling, tennis, and archery, attracted spectators chiefly interested in gambling. The cost of passing the time at such activities, as at dice and cards themselves, must remain problematical. No doubt it was high. Expense accounts of the time, recording gains and losses, yield familiar information: in the long run the amateur always lost.

When it comes to taverns and alehouses, we are on surer ground. In his *Survey* of 1603, Stow wrote, "quaffing . . .

---

[8] *Pierce Penilesse, His Supplication to the Divell* (1592), in McKerrow, ed., *Works*, I, 212.

[9] T. F., *Newes from the North* (1585), quoted in Graves, "Some References to Elizabethan Theaters," *Studies in Philology*, XIX (1922), 317.

[10] Nashe, *Christs Teares over Ierusalem* (1593) and *Pierce Penilesse, His Supplication to the Divell* (1592), in McKerrow, ed., *Works*, II, 148, and I, 217. Dekker also, as I recall, uses the phrase. Nashe (*Christs Teares over Ierusalem* [1593], in *ibid.*, II, 149) says that about a half crown is the "sette pryce of a strumpets soule" (i.e., first offense?).

is mightily encreased, though greatly qualified among the poorer sort, not of any holy abstinencie, but of meer necessitie, Ale and Beere being small, and Wines in price aboue their reach." [11] An afternoon in a tavern over a quart of sack—assuming that Falstaff's two gallons were not the normal requirement—would have cost our workman at least 8d. If he believed that a quart of ale was "a dish for a king," he could have had it at a minimum rate of 4d.; or if alehouse company would have compensated him for base drink, he could have had painfully small beer at 1d. a quart. A reckless bachelor, anxious to ape the gentry, might have smoked tobacco—at the rate of 3d. for each small pipeload.[12]

Dining in public might have appealed to some workman (or his wife) as an anniversary luxury. The threepenny ordinary is the cheapest I have encountered—for "your London Usurer, your stale Bachilor, and your thrifty Atturney . . . the roomes as full of company as a Iaile." [13] Observe that artisans were not looked for even in these niggardly surroundings. Sixpenny ordinaries were not lavish. Eightpenny ordinaries were, in 1631, for your country attorneys

[11] *Survey of London,* ed. Kingsford, I, 83.

[12] Sack cost 8d. a quart in London in 1595 (Rogers, *History of Agriculture and Prices in England,* VI, 415). Falstaff, paying 5s. 8d. for his two gallons, was not cheated, Shakespeare's prices being anachronistic. Sack at Eton in 1608 cost 11d. per quart (Beveridge, *Prices and Wages in England,* p. 113). In 1584, in spite of the injunction that ale or strong beer was to be sold at 1d. a quart, small beer at 1d. a pottle (2 quarts) in sealed measures, the actual selling price in Castle Baynard Ward was 3 farthings for a short pint ("Aleconners Complaint," in Stow, *Survey of London,* ed. Kingsford, I, lxiv–lxv). In 1614 Dame Ursla (Jonson's *Bartholomew Fair,* Act II, Scene ii) gets 6d. for a bottle of frothed ale, between 2d. and 3d. a quart for beer, and 3d. a pipeload for adulterated tobacco. She was a profiteer, but, except that her tobacco was mixed with coltsfoot, her charge for this item was not above average.

[13] Dekker, *Guls Horne-Booke* (1609), in Grosart, ed., *Non-Dramatic Works,* II, 244–45.

[58]

willing to "endure the Vnwholesome ayre." [14] Twelvepenny ordinaries were fashionable, and eighteenpenny ordinaries were, in 1592, for "Caualiers and braue courtiers." [15]

I shall add at random the cost of a few other nonessentials. Two printed broadsides, usually containing ballads, cost 1*d*., a prose romance of about 180 pages octavo 1*s*.,[16] a ride in a wherry from Paul's Wharf to Westminster 3*d*.,[17] more or less, depending on the waterman's powers in debate. The cheapest place in the private playhouse in Blackfriars could be had for 6*d*. We may now tabulate these prices, indicating the modern equivalents:

	Cost to Elizabethan Workman (Pence)	Cost to Modern Workman at Elizabethan Rates (Dollars)	Actual Cost of Modern Equivalent (Dollars)	
Low price, public theatre	1	.31		(Average
Middle price, public theatre	2	.62	.29	movie
High, but not highest, price, public theatre	3	.93		ticket)
Low price, private theatre	6	1.86	.55	(Theatre)
Quart of sack	8	2.48	1.25	**(Gin)**
Quart of ale	4	1.24	.20	(Beer)
Quart of small beer	1	.31		(No sale)
Pipeload of tobacco	3	.93	.01	
Cheapest dinner, table d'hôte	3	.93	.40	
Transportation fare	3	.93	.075	
Two printed sheets	1	.31	.03	(Newspaper)
Small book	12	3.72	.05	(Magazine)

[14] Thomas Powell, *Tom of All Trades* (1631), ed. Furnivall, New Shakspere Society Publications, Ser. VI, No. II, p. 141.

[15] Nashe, *Pierce Penilesse, His Supplication to the Divell* (1592), in McKerrow, ed., *Works*, I, 170.

[16] Plant, *English Book Trade*, p. 220.

[17] This was the official rate, and it seems to have been roughly adhered to: see "for Gibson . . . his boate hier four times between Lambeth and Ivy Bridge xii*d*." in Historical Manuscripts Commission, *Rutland MSS*, IV, 419–20.

That a penny was a considerable sum of money and that theatregoing was one of the few commercialized pleasures within the workman's means may readily be seen. In fact, the Elizabethan artisan paid so much more proportionately for necessities—food, clothing, fuel—that a penny for pleasure must have been more thoughtfully laid out than even its thirty-one cent equivalent need be at the present time. It is possible, however, that the high cost of living worked in favor of the theatres in one way: if the penny spent on food meant only an additional cucumber or two, one might as well squander it on a play. "Sights" in general were cheaper than material commodities in an age of scarcity. A penny fee would admit one to a puppet show,[18] a conducted tour of the monuments in Westminster Abbey, a view from the roof of St. Paul's Cathedral, a glimpse of a six-legged calf, or other "monster," or of the lions in the tower; by 1641, at least, it would purchase a stroll in a private garden where a nosegay was given as a souvenir.[19] But these were evanescent joys, to be tasted now and then, whereas beer, ballads, plays, and animal fights were staples. A play meant over two hours' entertainment in impressive surroundings—entertainment of a quality not to be found in the beer and ballads. Craftsmen, then, with their families, journeymen, and apprentices, must have composed the vast majority of "groundlings." Many were highly skilled, performing functions now allotted to the chemist, architect, and engineer. Let us not be too much influenced by contemptuous allusions to how the

[18] *Bartholomew Fair*, Act V, Scene i. Twopence were asked of "gentlefolk."
[19] Peacham, *Worth of a Penny* (1647 for 1641), in Arber, ed., *English Garner*, VI, 245–88.

"barmy Jacket of a Beer-brewer" [20] contaminated the public theatres. London craftsmen were the best in the country. Those at the Globe had chosen playgoing in preference to boozing and animalbaiting.

After the "Craftsmen" the next largest group in the London area was composed of the "Dealers and retailers." A few of these were merchants, wealthy and powerful, importing great cargoes and manipulating great sums. They would have been able to order without extravagance £10 dramatic performances in their homes. The greater number were, however, simply shopkeepers. In 1688 Gregory King reckoned the income of tradesmen as a class at only 12.5 percent higher than that of craftsmen. If the proportion held in 1601, the average shopkeeper earned 7s. 11d. weekly to the craftsman's 7s. and should have been grateful for penny admissions. Of course, many shopkeepers, and craftsmen too, could have afforded seats in the galleries and would have been pleased with the added penny's worth of comfort and dignity—especially when they brought their wives.

Among the "Gentry, professional men, and officials" the range of income was wide. In the professional group, teachers made least [21] (somewhat less than artisans), lawyers most. The witnesses are unanimous that in litigious London the lawyer prospered. Authors could make a living if they wrote for the stage. In 1599 about £35 passed into the hands of Thomas Dekker,[22] as compared with £18 4s. for the average

[20] Marston, *Jack Drum's Entertainment* (1600), Act V, Scene i, in Wood, ed., *Plays*.

[21] Plant, *English Book Trade*, p. 42.

[22] *Henslowe's Diary*, ed. Greg, I, 100–117. Some payments may not be recorded.

artisan, but Dekker wrote in that year all of three plays and parts of six more. "Gentry," of course, is scarcely an occupational term. Those who were not professional men, officials, or heads of their own households were usually "serving men"—attendants at court or in the households of nobles or other gentlemen. Since living was provided, stipends in most cases may be considered as spending money. Dekker speaks of "bare forty shillings a yeere (seruing-mens wages),"[23] and when we consider that a groom of the chamber for Queen Elizabeth received £2 13s. 4d., the rate seems not improbable. On the other hand, Elizabeth's gentlemen of the privy chamber received £50 and perquisites.[24] Forty shillings a year meant nine pence and a farthing in weekly spending money. The twopenny gallery, for all its bourgeois flavor, might well have been considered expensive enough by the younger or lesser gentry. Money was scarce among the majority of all classes. I am not speaking, to be sure, of the income of elder sons who had come into their estates. I am not speaking, either, of knights, baronets, and temporal lords. But of these no more than a sprinkling could be looked for in any audience: there weren't enough in all England to fill the Globe.

A great lord was expected to pay more for all things than lesser men. There follows a few illustrative items from the personal expense account of the Earl of Rutland in 1598–99:

Item for Sir Ph. Sidneys *Arcadia* [3d ed.?], ixs.
Item for my Lorde's supper at Courte, 28 *Octoberis*, ixs. iid.
 . . . the cooke in the pryvy kitchen, xs. . . . tobacco pipes, viiid.

[23] *Worke for Armourours* (1609), in Grosart, ed., *Non-Dramatic Works*, IV, 130.
[24] Chambers, *Elizabethan Stage*, I, 50.

Item, 28 September, my Lorde's boatehier to Lambeth and back
againe, xviii*d*. . . . boatehire 1 October, for his Lordship
and his men, and the play, and James his going to Lambeth
to see Capten Whitlock, viii*s*.

Item the foteman's boatehire to Lambeth and to the play howse
sondry tymes, ii*s*. iiii*d*.

Item, 28 *Julii*, an oz. of ball tobacco, v*s*.; boatehier for his Lordship that day, xii*d*.; to the buttery at Nonesuch, v*s*.

Item, 18 November, for an oz of tobacco, ii*s*. vi*d*. . . . boatehier and a play, vi*s*.[25]

Playhouse prices were not designed for earls. Although his
lordship seems to have paid above the highest rate, plays
were still the least of his extravagances. It appears that on
one occasion a regular theatre party for himself and an
unspecified number of retainers, besides boat hire and miscel-
laneous expenses, cost Rutland only 8*s*., or 3*s*. more than he
later paid for one ounce of tobacco, 2*s*. less than he had
previously tipped the queen's cook.

Descending now to the opposite end of the scale, to those
below the rank of artisan—to the carman, the peddler, the
ditcher, and the household drudge—most of these could
have found a holiday penny not urgently needed to keep
body and soul together:

Nay many poore pincht, needie creatures, that liue of almes, and
that haue scarce neither cloath to their backe, nor foode for the
belley, yet wil make hard shift but they will see a Play, let wife
& children begge, languish in penurie, and all they can rappe and
rend, is little enough to lay vpon such vanitie.[26]

But their numbers at any one performance would have been
limited indeed.

[25] Historical Manuscripts Commission, *Rutland MSS*, IV, 419–20.
[26] Crosse, *Vertues Common-Wealth; or, The High-Way to Honour*
(1603), signature Q^v.

Any amusement over the admission prices to Shakespeare's theatre is apt to disappear upon a scrutiny of the facts. Actually the 1*d.*, 2*d.*, and 3*d.* range, with a few removed places at 6*d.* and 12*d.*, was designed to fit the purses of London. These prices were truly popular. The only improvement one might have suggested would have been additional places at a farthing. Cheap labor and high prices insure great profits and stimulate commercial enterprise; periods of "price inflation" have been accredited with various triumphs, including, whimsically one supposes, the plays of Shakespeare. It is true that the theatres were built in the midst of that period of expansion marked by high prices and low wages, but the theatrical industry, before the advent of the "private" theatres, may be pointed out as an exception to, as well as an exemplification of, the inflationary tendencies of the period. Admission prices were calculated, as prices in general were not, to what workmen could afford to pay. We must conclude, first, that audiences were composed largely of shopkeepers and craftsmen, people of low income taking advantage of the almost unique opportunity to get their money's worth; and, second, that those who limited their expenditure to 1*d.* and remained "groundlings" must not be thought of as a rabble. Another thing is certain. When the "private" theatres opened and placed the minimum charge at 6*d.*, no more effective means could have been devised for excluding utterly the great majority of the former audience. This was price inflation with a vengeance. The thrifty citizen who has blundered into Salisbury Court Theatre in 1629 is made to say:

> I will hasten to the money Box
> And take my shilling out again, for now

I have considered that it is too much;
I'll go to th' Bull, or Fortune, and there see
A Play for two pense, with a Jig to boot.[27]

He is portrayed as ridiculous, but he was completely right: a shilling was indeed too much. And the price inflation at the private theatres begat no second Shakespeare.

Factors other than expense affect theatrical attendance. That only two in fifteen Elizabethan Londoners went to the theatre weekly, as compared with the ten in fifteen modern Americans who go to the movies, was partly due to the scarcity of pennies. It was partly due also to the scarcity of leisure. Plays were performed, not two or three times a day, at the public's convenience, but usually only once, and then during working hours. Drama competed with labor in the use of daylight, and opportunity for playgoing was accordingly limited. In our day, many housewives and young people during the afternoon, and workers generally during the evening, are free agents. Shakespeare's actors had to look forward to holidays, and theatres were built huge to accommodate holiday crowds. The analogy between the modern movie and the Elizabethan theatre is in many ways a poor one. Mechanical reproduction now makes possible a constantly varied bill. In any city and in most towns one may go to the movies every day in the week without seeing the same picture twice. In "Middletown" with a population of between thirty-five and forty thousand, nine movies were offering twenty-two programs and three hundred performances each week in 1923.[28] Our eighty-five million weekly spectators are made up largely of those who go from two to

[27] Praeludium, *The Careless Shepherdess.*
[28] Lynd and Lynd, *Middletown*, p. 263.

[65]

four times a week.[29] In Shakespeare's time, one visit a week would more than have exhausted the possibilities of the theatres so far as mere novelty was concerned. We live in an age of expert salesmanship, and, whereas Elizabethans had to go to the theatres, the movies come to us. There are seventeen thousand movie theatres in the United States— roofed, comfortably heated (sometimes even cooled), and usually "palatial." This means about one theatre for every 7,647 inhabitants. To equal these facilities, London of the year of *Hamlet* would have needed over twenty "neighborhood" theatres dotting every locality from Lambeth to Mile End.[30] Actually there were four in operation, rigidly restricted to particular districts. London was small in area; nevertheless, the average citizen had to walk more than a mile to reach the Rose or the Globe. The distance from St. Paul's Cathedral was about a mile and a half; from Wapping, two miles; from St. James Clerkenwell, over two miles; from Westminster, three miles and a half. Of course, one might ride the Thames, but that meant additional expense.

Standards of convenience are, however, relative. Official London considered the theatres damnably convenient, and unofficial London considered them commodious and magnificent. "Commedies," lamented Gosson, "are neither chargable to ye beholders purse, nor painful to his body; partly, because he may sit out of the raine to viewe the same, when

[29] Although eighty-five million attend the movies weekly, only forty million, about 30 percent of our population, are said to "really have the movie habit." See Thorp, *America at the Movies*, p. 3.

[30] They were larger, of course, than the average movie theatre. A seat is said to be available for every twelve Americans. In the theatres operating in 1601, I should say that there was a space available for every twenty-three Londoners.

many other pastimes are hindred by wether." [31] Under
harder conditions of life, mere shelter may seem a luxury.
The conflict of playtime with working hours was the more
serious obstacle. Nashe speaks of "the after-noone beeing
the idlest time of the day; wherein men that are their owne
masters (as Gentlemen of the Court, the Innes of the Courte,
and the number of Captaines and Souldiers about London)
do wholy bestow themselues vpon pleasure." [32] The vast
majority did not belong to this select company. Shopkeepers
to a degree were their own masters, workmen less so, although not so completely regimented by time clocks as now.
The workday varied in length from about eight hours in
midwinter to about twelve hours in midsummer, consisting
of the period of clear daylight with dinnertime and drinking
time off. [33] Possibly one could pool his time off and use it
to go to the theatre. The leathersellers agreed that work
was to cease early on Saturdays, vigils, and festivals. [34] Vigils
and festivals were many, and they varied for various crafts;
the various crafts imitated the practice if not the precept of
the leathersellers. Individual workmen had their private
holidays, and there were intermissions between one job and
the next. Beyond a certain point restraint upon human conduct becomes impossible. That they drew workmen from
their work was one of the chief of the official counts against
plays. Schoolboys and apprentices must have been given, or
must have taken, their times of recreation. We may assume

[31] *Playes Confuted in Fiue Actions* (1582), in Hazlitt, ed., *English
Drama and Stage*, p. 202.
[32] *Pierce Penilesse, His Supplication to the Divell* (1592), in McKerrow, ed., *Works*, I, 212.
[33] Knoop and Jones, *Mediaeval Mason*, p. 236.
[34] Dunlop, *English Apprenticeship and Child Labour*, p. 45.

that the idler classes formed a higher percentage of audiences than of the population generally but never that they composed more than a minority.

Personal and religious scruples kept some Londoners away from the theatres but fewer than we are apt to suppose. If the theatres were respectable enough to be frequented by the Earl of Rutland and his class, we might assume that the average citizen would not shrink from them; however, it may be best to make no assumptions about the sense of propriety of the English middle classes. Actually there has been much misunderstanding about the association of the playhouses with brothels and about their location in the sinister suburbs. If there were playhouses in the suburbs, there were also numerous churches; certainly the wardens of St. Saviour's did not think the neighborhood of Southwark a blight upon the drama.[35] If there were brothels in Shoreditch and Southwark, there were brothels also elsewhere. The royal suburb of Westminster was notorious for them. The slums were in the suburbs, but the suburbs were not the slums. Many substantial households were established there. A dweller in the intramural city who refused to go into them would have been a virtual prisoner, cut off from the innocent pleasures of the open fields and from much of his everyday business. The intramural city itself was not uniformly a place for the fastidious.

Religious scruples require a more extended consideration. It is certain that an increasing number of Londoners stayed away from plays on moral and religious grounds and that this number by 1642 had become formidable. The strict

[35] For their protest against the presence of the theatres, see Chambers, *Elizabethan Stage*, IV, 325.

Calvinist William Perkins had more delicate consciences in his keeping than any other Elizabethan, and Perkins had decided that plays were not permissible.[36] This particular venality, I should say however, drew fire only from his lighter artillery. So far as I can discover, nothing ever came of the attempt, partly inspired by pressure from the pulpits, to force masters and wardens of the London companies to forbid their apprentices, servants, and journeymen to go to plays; [37] nor have I ever heard of articles of apprenticeship outlawing playgoing, although cardplaying and tavern-haunting were invariably forbidden. The very strict regulations of the Merchant Adventurers of Bristol forbidding apprentices to "daunce dice carde mum or use any musick eyther by night or day in the streetes" [38] are silent about the mere witnessing of amusements. The very shrillness of the pulpit attacks upon playgoing suggests frustration. The people found the ministers "sumwhat too sour in preaching awey theyr pastime." We can hear them argue back:

they wil saie, you are a man of the Sabboth you are verie precise; you wil allowe vs nothing; you wil haue nothing but the worde of God: you wil permit vs no recreation, but haue men like Asses, who neuer rest but when they are eating.

Seeke to withdrawe these felowes from the Theater vnto the sermon, they wil saie, By the preacher they maie be edified, but by the plaier both edified and delighted.[39]

---

[36] "Cases of Conscience," *The Workes of that Famous and Worthy Minister of Christ in the University of Cambridge, Mr. William Perkins* (1613), II, 140.

[37] "Dramatic Records of the City of London: the Repertories, Journals, and Letter Books," in *Malone Society Collections*, II, Part III, 313.

[38] Dunlop, *English Apprenticeship and Child Labour*, p. 189.

[39] *Second and Third Blast of Retrait from Plaies and Theaters* (1580), in Hazlitt, ed., *English Drama and Stage*, pp. 139–40.

Comparison of plays with sermons as edification the preachers found especially infuriating. The people must have found equally so the preachers' tendency to define recreation as the fifteen-minute rest periods allowed to harvesters.

The preachers themselves, individual pietists, and small congregations of sectaries—small, that is, in Shakespeare's time and in London—would have stayed away from plays on religious grounds, but not the rank and file of otherwise faithful parishioners. An analogy may be found in the habits of the eight million American Methodists who, until it was recently amended, honored their "Discipline" (forbidding dancing and cardplaying) chiefly in the breach. We must concede, of course, that Puritanism is no longer a rising tide. Milton had no objection to the well-trod stage, to Jonson's learned sock, and to Shakespeare's wood-notes wild. The attitude of John Chamberlain toward worldly vanities was stiff, and, when he saw Tobie Matthew on his way to a play, he thought that "playeng and Fridayes fasting agree not so well together as prayeing in a man of so much profession." [40] Yet he himself was not "so sowre nor severe" but that he would unbend occasionally: in 1597, when the new "play of humors" was "in very great request," he "was drawn alonge to yt by the common applause"; [41] and, in 1614, hearing that the rebuilt Globe playhouse was the "fayrest that ever was in England," he planned to look in at it.[42]

Tobie Matthew was a Roman Catholic convert, his conduct an object of general interest. Like their fellow nonconformists, the extreme Puritans, the Catholics were expected to adhere to the strict way of life. Amusing evidence

[40] February 7, 1618. *Letters of John Chamberlain*, ed. McClure, II, 137.

[41] *Ibid.*, I, 32.　　　　　　[42] *Ibid.*, p. 544.

of their attitude toward the theatres exists in manuscript.[43] On March 9, 1617 [1618?], William Harrison, Archpriest, "Forasmuch as there haue been seuerall complaincts made, & aduertisement giuen, that not a few are scanalised, and more disedified by the goeing of certain Priests to playes, acted by common plaiers upon common stages" prohibited "all, & euery" of the priests under his direction from going to the theatres on penalty of the loss of "his or theyr faculties." On April 25, 1618, one Thomas Leke protested, raising the issue of "Ecclesiastical libertie" and objecting that the prohibition ran "generallie against all plaies, & not rather with a limitation against scurril playes, or wherein religion is disgraced." This drew forth a rejoinder, presumably from Harrison. It is lengthy and partly *ad hominem*. He says that the prohibition was put in general terms only to save the face of Leke himself, with two other chief offenders, Mr. Thules and Mr. Canon. He explains that the prohibition was against "going to theatres," not against "seeing plays," and that attendance at performances at court, the universities, the Inns of Court, and gentlemen's houses was not forbidden. Of public performances he is more than distrustful:

For such playes are made to sport, and delight the auditorie, which consisting most of young gallants, and Protestants (for no true Puritanes will endure to bee present at playes) how unlikely is it, but that there are, and must bee, at least some passages in the playes, which may relish, and tickle the humor of such persons, or else good night to the players.[44]

---

[43] Manuscript in the Folger Shakespeare Library: Prohibition of William Harison, Archpriest, wherein English secular priests are forbidden to attend the theatres, March 9, 1617, with Thomas Leke's protest against the prohibition, April 25, 1618, and Harison's (?) answer to Leke.

[44] Folio 13.

Harrison was obviously a practical thinker. Leke had observed that the Jesuits and Benedictines made no objection to plays and that: "Wee knowe, that most of the principal Catholicks about London doe goe to playes, and all for ye most part of my ghostly children do knowe that I sometimes goe, and are not scandalised." To which Harrison rejoined: "the Catholicks that use to playes are the young of both sexes, and neither matrons, nor graue, or sage man is there seen." On this note of conflict in the testimony we must leave the matter, recognizing, however, that Father Leke had a more intimate knowledge of audiences than had Father Harrison. We know of one "ghostly child" who went to the playhouse and was there subjected to the amorous attentions of no less a person than the Venetian ambassador.[45] She must have been young, but Tobie Matthew was past fifty and an ordained priest on that fasting day when Chamberlain met him on his way to the theatre.

On moral grounds the theatres were defended as well as attacked—as well they might have been in view of the general character of the plays and of the freedom of the premises from gambling, the national vice. Taverns and alehouses were afflicted with dicing and cardplaying; sporting events, even bowling and tennis matches, with betting. Drunkenness was already a common vice. We learn from the Overburian characters that only the playhouses can keep the waterman sober; [46] from Nashe, that only the playhouses can heal the debauchee:

Faith, when Dice, Lust, and Drunkennesse, and all haue dealt vpon him, if there be neuer a Playe for him to goe too for his

---

[45] Public Record Office, *Calendar of State Papers, Venice and Northern Italy, 1615–1617*, XIV, 593.

[46] Overbury, *Overburian Characters*, Percy Reprints, No. XIII, p. 68.

pennie, he sits melancholie in his Chamber, deuising vpon felonie or treason, and howe he may best exalt himselfe by mischiefe.[47]

Heywood's *Apology for Actors* bases its defence partly upon the grounds of public morality, and each of the writers of commendatory verses for the volume comes forth with his personal testimonial:

> Have I not knowne a man, that to be hyr'd
> Would not for any treasure see a play,
> Reele from a taverne?

asks Robert Pallant.

> Thou that do'st raile at me for seeing a play,
> How wouldst thou have me spend my idle houres?
> Wouldst have me in a taverne drinke all day?
>
> .   .   .   .
>
> To drabbe, to game, to drinke, all these I hate,

says Richard Perkins, who affirms moreover that he is proud to sit "even in the stages front" where all may see him. Arthur Pallant is even more emphatic:

> To call to church Campanus bels did make;
> Playes, dice and drink invite men to forsake.[48]

The professional moralists were unwilling to make concessions; one of them, nevertheless, after showing scant regard for the theatres, is forced to conclude: "notwithstanding, if we marke how young men spend the latter end of the day in gaming, drinking, whoring, it were better to tollerate Playes."[49] We must be careful not to assume that the

---

[47] *Pierce Penilesse, His Supplication to the Divell* (1592), in McKerrow, ed., *Works*, I, 214.

[48] Heywood, *Apology for Actors* (1612), Shakespeare Society Publications, No. III, pp. 8–11.

[49] Joseph Wyburne, *New Age of Old Names* (1609), p. 53.

theatres were the particular haunt of the irreligious or the debased.

Neither cost, nor inconvenience, nor a belief that the playhouses were contaminative would have kept large sectors of the populace from plays. What of delicacy or shyness, such as might be supposed to influence the habits of women? It is surprising, in view of the evidence to the contrary, how many authoritative works convey the impression that few women went to the Elizabethan public theatres. We read in A. W. Ward that "no respectable woman might appear at a playhouse except with her face concealed under a mask." [50] Now it is certain that women generally did not wear masks at the plays. In Restoration times wearing masks became common and allusions to them legion. In Elizabethan times allusions are hard to find—an unlikely concomitant of so conspicuous and vulnerable a custom—and such few as exist do not associate masks with respectability.[51] We read in Ashley H. Thorndike that at Shakespeare's first play "the galleries contained a fair proportion of women" (the galleries only?) and that "in the early days . . . there were few women and no young girls." [52] I do not know to what early days the statement can apply. Even before the regular theatres were built, the audiences in London innyards were said to offer occasion for "inveglynge and alleurynge of maides speciallye orphanes, and good Cityzens Children vnder Age, to previe and vnmete Contractes," [53] and in 1579 Gosson's

---

[50] *History of English Dramatic Literature*, I, 477.

[51] It is "the light-taylde huswiues," the sirens and Circes, who wear masks at the "Bank-sides round-house" in John Lane's *Tom Tell-Troths Message, and His Pens Complaint* (1600), ed. Furnivall, New Shakespeare Society Publications, Ser. VI, No. II, p. 133.

[52] *Shakespeare's Theater*, pp. 404, 409.

[53] "Dramatic Records from the Lansdowne Manuscripts," in *Malone Society Collections*, I, Part II, 175.

Schoole of Abuse contained a special epistle "To the Gentle-women Citizens of London" beseeching them to withdraw their patronage from plays. We read in Sir Edmund Chambers that: "The galleries were full of light women who found them a profitable haunt, but whose presence did not altogether prevent that of ladies of position, probably in the private rooms, and possibly masked." [54] Wholly disregarded here is a feminine category, large in any age we trust, composed of neither "ladies of position" nor "light women." Either there is a lode of information uncited and unknown to me, or the authorities have decided that Shakespeare's theatre was no place for a lady and are imposing their own sense of decorum upon the Elizabethans.

The "light women" will concern us in the next chapter. At the moment we shall consider those who merit a presumption of innocence, who came from all classes of society, and who sometimes may have stood in the pit, side by side with their menfolk although all naturally would prefer the galleries. That there were women in the pit is suggested by one of Robert Greene's anecdotes of 1592. A young "nip" is in a packed theatre observing the technique of a master cutpurse. The youth, the expert, and a young woman are pressed close among "a company of seemly men":

In short time the deed [stealing the purse] was performed, but how, the young nip could not easily discern, only he felt him shift his hand toward his trug, to convey the purse to her, but she, being somewhat mindful of the play, because a merriment was then on the stage, gave no regard.[55]

---

[54] *Elizabethan Stage*, II, 549.
[55] *Thirde and Last Part of Connycatching* (1592), in Judges, ed., *Elizabethan Underworld*, p. 195.

The "nip," less susceptible to the appeal of drama, substituted his own hand and edged off with the purse. Now, unless there had been other women among the throng, the value of the "trug" as receiver would have been nil. My representative of female groundlings is none too respectable, but I am thinking of those who covered her presence.

In London the women outnumbered men thirteen to ten, although more than the reverse would have been true in the upper crust.[56] There were fewer than thirty women among Queen Elizabeth's fifteen hundred courtiers,[57] and in the Inns of Court and among fashionable sojourners males of course predominated. Some of the male courtiers, to be sure, had families established in Westminster or London; the women of fashion were numerous enough, and their numbers rapidly increasing. English women, high and low, were great "gadders abroad." On this point natives and foreigners agreed. Chamberlain writes dryly to Alice Carleton that he has tried to see her married sister twice, but the first time she was away at a neighbor's house playing cards, the second time at the Globe.[58] England, said the foreigners, was "a woman's paradise." Platter describes how "they have more liberty than in other lands, and know how to make good use of it," going constantly abroad while "the men must put up with such ways, and may not punish them for

[56] I assume that the proportion at the end of the century (see Gregory King, "Natural and Political Observations," in Barnett, ed., *Two Tracts by Gregory King*, p. 22) held good for the beginning. King refines his analysis further: husbands and wives, 37 percent; widows and widowers (mostly widows then as now), 9 percent; children, 33 percent; servants, 13 percent; sojourners, etc., 8 percent.

[57] Cheyney, *History of England*, I, 18–19, 47.

[58] June 30, 1614. *Letters of John Chamberlain*, ed. McClure, I, 544.

it." [59] It is hard to believe his statement that "what is particularly curious is that the women as well as the men, in fact more often than they, will frequent the taverns or alehouses for enjoyment." [60]

Whatever their attitude toward taverns, the women of London displayed little shyness about going to theatres. It is for the wives and daughters of ordinary citizens that Stephen Gosson was especially concerned in 1579. When he says finally, "I have seene many of you whiche were wont to sporte your selues, at Theaters, when you perceiued the abuse of those places, schoole your selues, and of your owne accorde abhorre Playes," [61] he is resorting to cajolery. Female attendance did not fall off, and in 1617 Robert Anton wrote bitterly of the theatres' attracting "Swarmes of Wiues." [62] The most objective descriptions of Elizabethan theatres have come to us from foreign visitors, and on one subject these visitors were agreed. Said Platter in 1599:

With these and many more amusements the English pass their time, learning at the play what is happening abroad; *indeed men and womenfolk visit such places without scruple,* since the English for the most part do not travel much, but prefer to learn foreign matters and take their pleasures at home. [63]

And Philip Julius in 1602:

there are always a good many people present, *including many respectable women* [*auch viele ehrbare Frauens*] because use-

---

[59] *Thomas Platter's Travels in England, 1599,* pp. 181–82.
[60] *Ibid.,* p. 170.
[61] *Schoole of Abuse* (1579), ed. Arber, English Reprints, No. III, p. 58.
[62] *Vices Anotimie Scourged and Corrected,* cited in Graves, "Notes on Puritanism and the Stage," *Studies in Philology,* XVIII (1921), 146.
[63] *Thomas Platter's Travels in England, 1599,* p. 170 (italics mine).

ful arguementa, and many good doctrines, as we were told, are brought forward there.[64]

And Father Busino in 1614:

These theatres are frequented by a number of respectable and handsome ladies, who come freely and seat themselves among the men without the slightest hesitation.[65]

The second statement applies to the public as well as the private theatres, the first and third specifically to public theatres. Together they seem to me conclusive. The proportion of men and women is now irrecoverable, but it is worth noting that the only contemporary "sampling" of an audience which has survived—a casualty list after the collapse of Paris Garden in 1583—yields five men, four women, and one child.[66] They were assembled at a bearbaiting.

Young men and maids, husbands and wives, went to the theatres together, sometimes in family parties. The ground lease for the earliest of the theatres stipulated that, provided "Gyles [Alleyn] hys wyfe and familie doe com and take ther places before they shalbe taken vpp by any others," [67] they might see any play free of charge. Jonson's *Every Man out of His Humor* (1599) offers a sop, uncommon with the writer, to the "graue, wise citizen, or modest matron" [68] lest they take offense at the portrait of Deliro and his wife. Examples might be multiplied. No one need be reminded

---

[64] "Diary of the Journey of Philip Julius, Duke of Stettin-Pomerania, through England in the Year 1602," eds. G. von Bülow and W. Powell, in *Royal Historical Society Transactions*, New Series, VI, 29 (italics mine).

[65] "Diaries and Despatches of the Venetian Embassy at the Court of King James I, in the Years 1617, 1618," *Quarterly Review*, CII (1857), 416 (italics mine).

[66] The list is given on p. 84.

[67] Chambers, *Elizabethan Stage*, II, 387.   [68] Grex, Act II.

of George the Grocer, Goodwife Nell, and Ralph the Apprentice in *The Knight of the Burning Pestle.*

About 20 percent of the metropolitan population was under ten years of age, about 30 percent under sixteen years of age.[69] A few children would have been taken to the theatres by their parents, but it is doubtful if many could have commanded both the freedom and the penny that would make them independent playgoers until they were sixteen—the age at which girls were marriageable and boys ready to enter their apprenticeship. If we let the age at which Londoners began going to plays hover between ten and sixteen, we eliminate 25 percent of the population and come upon the first major restriction upon a concept of the audience as a mere cross section of London humanity. The restriction does not lessen the probability that Shakespeare's audience was youthful. It was about as true in 1601 as in 1696 that "the Males & Females in the Kingdome in General are Aged one with another 27½ years." [70] Mean ages are, however, deceptive at best and especially so in those earlier times when such large numbers failed to survive childhood. There are better reasons for speaking of the youthfulness of Shakespeare's audience.

Standing for several hours or bustling for a place in the galleries would have diminished in appeal as a man grew older. At a popular play one could obtain a good place only

[69] I base this percentage on the figures of King, "Natural and Political Observations," in Barnett, ed., *Two Tracts by Gregory King,* pp. 22–23. The child population in London was smaller per capita than in the rest of the kingdom, so that I have modified the percentages obtainable in the table at the head of p. 23 according to the proportions indicated for "children" in London and in the rest of the kingdom in the table at the foot of p. 22.

[70] "Natural and Political Observations," in Barnett, ed., *Two Tracts by Gregory King,* p. 23.

by coming early and enduring a long wait. The arduousness
of playgoing rather than the frivolity seems to have acted as
a restraint upon the elderly John Chamberlain. The drama,
in any case, has always made its first call to youth. Two
groups are mentioned again and again in contemporary allusions to the theatres—the students of the Inns of Court
and the apprentices of London.

London was the third university city of the kingdom.
About 1595 we hear that

> the clamorous frie of Innes of Court
> Filles vp the priuate roomes of greater prise: [71]

Before and after 1595, we come upon constant reminders that
the plays were a magnet for the students. The number of
these was not great. In 1574 there were 593 students in the
four Inns, in addition to the 51 benchers and 125 utter
barristers.[72] In the reign of James the number had risen to
about 720 students, in addition to about 80 benchers and 240
utter barristers.[73] But it was not unusual for the students to
have young friends and relatives lodging with them, and
what the group lacked in total numbers was counterbalanced
by the large proportion of those numbers possessing the
money, leisure, and inclination for playgoing. A student at
the Inns of Court was a well-born, affluent, university-edu-
cated young man in his earlier twenties. He lived in a society devoted to intellectual pursuits and well disposed
towards belles-lettres. He must have made a good spectator.

---

[71] Sir John Davies, "In Sillam," Epigram No. 28, in Grosart, ed.,
Complete Poems, II, 27–28.
[72] *Calendar of Inner Temple Records*, ed. Inderwick, I, 468–69.
[73] Wheatley, *London, Past and Present*, II, 261.

We cannot generalize too far, of course, and an epigram by
Davies will serve to shade our portrait:

Publius student at the Common-law
Oft leaves his Bookes, and for his recreation,
To Paris-garden doth himselfe withdrawe,
Where he is rauisht with such delectation,
As downe among the beares and dogges he goes;
Where, whilst he skipping cries "to head to head,"
His satten doublet and his veluet hose
Are all with spittle from aboue be-spread.[74]

Turning now from gown to town, we must recognize that
the apprentices of London would have outnumbered the
students ten to one. They had no income except what spending money was allowed them by parents or masters, and
theoretically they had no weekday leisure, but by hook or
crook they flocked to the theatres. Their tastes are often
supposed to be reflected in Jonson's familiar lines:

He rather prayes, you will be pleas'd to see
One such, to day, as other playes should be.
Where neither Chorus wafts you ore the seas,
Nor creaking throne comes downe the boyes to please; [75]

and their habits in accounts like the following:

The little devils are the apprentices, alias shopboys, who, on
two days of the year, which prove fatal to them, Shrove Tuesday and the first of May, are so riotous and outrageous, that
in a body, three or four thousand strong, they go committing

---

[74] "In Publium," Epigram No. 43, in Grosart, ed., *Complete Poems*,
II, 40–41.
[75] Prologue, *Every Man in His Humor* (1598), in Herford and Simpson, eds., *Ben Jonson*.

excesses in every direction, killing human beings and demolishing houses." [76]

This portrait has too much shade. The Shrove Tuesday riot of 1617, for which the apprentice saturnalia furnished only a pretext, explains the horrified tone of the writer. Normally apprentices were well behaved: they had to be.

Apprentices were not all "boyes." They were compelled by statute to be twenty-four years of age before coming out of their apprenticeship, so that most of those in London were between seventeen and twenty-four—single, native-born, and mentally and physically fit. They formed, indeed, a superior class. The sons of unskilled laborers and husbandmen were generally barred from apprenticeship, and certain guilds insisted upon property qualifications in the parents and educational qualifications in the boy. Gentle birth was not uncommon. The apprentices were lodged with householders; they were soberly dressed (with cropped hair) and compelled to walk a chalk line.[77] But in London they walked with the pride of possession: some of them would become lord mayors, dining magnificently foreign noblemen and receiving visits in state by the Archbishop of Canterbury. Many of them, perhaps the majority, had about as much formal education as Shakespeare himself. They, like the students, should have made pretty good spectators. One of the bourgeois traits of Beaumont's apprentice, Ralph, is that he recites at length from Shakespeare—with somewhat

[76] "Diaries and Despatches of the Venetian Embassy at the Court of King James I, in the years 1617, 1618," *Quarterly Review*, CII (1857), 413–14.
[77] Dunlop, *English Apprenticeship and Child Labour*, pp. 52, 55–56.

fewer errors than would be made by a modern college student. The term "apprentice," of course, is loosely used to designate all the boys of London, among whom no doubt there were plenty of ragamuffins.

We have now glanced at all of the major factors controlling theatrical attendance—save one. None of these factors except that of age can be said conclusively to have kept from the theatres more than a fraction of the available public. Together they help to explain why only two in fifteen Londoners went to the theatres weekly, but they fail to explain why from sixty to seventy thousand "adult" Londoners never went to the theatres at all.[78] The explanation of that phenomenon lies in the one factor not hitherto examined. It is obvious enough. Many people stayed away from the theatres because they did not care for plays. A dramatic and poetic age confers no universal taste for poetry and drama. Elizabethans could be Philistines, and thousands of them were.

Purely external considerations argue for the heterogeneity of the audience, for little selection on the basis of class, occupation, sex, respectability (or its opposite), and the like. The argument is sustained by the cataloguing descriptions of the audiences which the age produced. I shall set these down without comment, asking the reader to take each with reserve, in view of the angry or satirical mood of the speakers, but to let all together form the synthesis:

[78] Taking the estimated population of 160,000 in 1605 and subtracting 25 percent for the underage group leaves 120,000. Subtracting the probable number of playgoers, no greater in 1605 than 50,000 to 60,000 (see pp. 43–44), we have 60,000 to 70,000 left.

Anno 1582

the common people which resorte to Theatres being but an assemblie of Tailers, Tinkers, Cordwayners, Saylers, olde Men, yong Men, Women, Boyes, Girles, and such like.[79]

Anno 1583

Mentioned as killed, injured, or miraculously saved when Paris Garden collapsed while a thousand people were watching a bearbaiting on Sunday:

Adam Spencer, a felmonger of Southwark.

William Cockram, a baker of Shoreditch.

John Burton, a clerk of St. Marie Wolmers in Lombard St.

Mathew Mason, a servant with Master Garland of Southwark.

Thomas Peace, a servant with Rob. Tasker of Clerkenwell.

Alice White, a servant to a pursemaker without Cripplegate.

Marie Harrison, daughter to John, a water-bearer of Lombard St.

Mrs. Webb, wife of a pewterer of Limestreet.

An unidentified woman and her small child.[80]

Anno 1595

For, as we see at all the play-house doores,
When ended is the play, the dance, and song,
A thousand Townesmen, gentlemen, and whores,
Porters and serving-men together throng.[81]

Anno 1597

They are the ordinary places for vagrant persons, Maisterles men, thieves, horse stealers, whoremongers, Coozeners, Conycatchers, contrivers of treason and other idele and daungerous persons to meet together. . . . They maintaine idlenes in such

---

[79] Gosson, *Playes Confuted in Fiue Actions*, in Hazlitt, ed., *English Drama and Stage*, p. 184.

[80] John Field, *A Godly Exhortation*, quoted in Chambers, *Elizabethan Stage*, IV, 220.

[81] Sir John Davies, "In Cosmun," Epigram No. 17, in Grosart, ed., *Complete Poems*, II, 18.

persons as haue no vocation & draw apprentices and other seruants from theire ordinary workes and all sorts of people from the resort vnto sermons and other Christian exercises to the great hinderance of traides & pphanation of religion.[82]

Anno 1608

The wise, and many headed Bench, that sits
Upon the Life and Death of playes, and Wits,
Compos'd of Gamester, Captain, Knight, Knight's man,
Lady or Pusill that wears mask or fan,
Velvet, or Taffata cap, rank'd in the dark
With the shops Foreman, or some such brave spark.[83]

Anno 1609

[Dramatic cakes]
fit for ladies: some for lords, knights, squires,
Some for your waiting wench, and city-wires,
Some for your men, and daughters of white-Friars.[84]

Anno 1624

I doubt not but you have heard of our famous play of Gondomar, which hath been followed with extraordinarie concourse, and frequented by all sorts of people old and younge, rich and poore, masters and servants, papists and puritans, wise men *et ct.*, churchmen and statesmen as Sir Henry Wotton, Sir Albert Morton, Sir Benjamin Ruddier, Sir Thomas Lake, and a world besides; the Lady Smith wold have gon yf she could have persuaded me to go with her. I am not so sowre nor severe but that I wold willingly have attended her, but I could not sit so long, for we must have ben there before one a clocke at farthest to find any roome.[85]

---

[82] "Dramatic Records of the City of London: the Remembrancia," in *Malone Society Collections*, I, Part I, 80.

[83] Jonson's commendatory verses to *The Faithful Shepherdess*.

[84] Prologue, *Epicoene* (1609), in Herford and Simpson, eds., *Ben Jonson*.

[85] Chamberlain to Carleton, August 21. See *Letters of John Chamberlain*, ed. McClure, II, 577–78.

[Plays are] First for strangers, who can desire no better recreation than to come and see a play: then for Citizens to feast their wits: then for Gallants who otherwise perhaps would spend their money in drunkennesse and lasciviousnesse, [and] doe find a great delight and delectation to see a Play: then for the learned it does increase and adde wit constructively to wit: then for Gentlewomen, it teacheth them how to deceive idlenesse: then for the ignorant it does augment their knowledge.[86]

The descriptions fused into one composite portrait give us, I believe, the truth about the kind of people in Shakespeare's audience. If the descriptions seem to make the type of spectators appear more genteel as time passes, it is partly because of the accident that some of the later writers were thinking primarily about that portion of the general theatrical public patronizing "private" theatres after 1599, more of which in a moment. The last description mentions a category of playgoers numerically few but of considerable interest: the "strangers." London was renowned through Europe for its theatres, and foreign visitors always saw a play or two, even when they could not understand the language. "Playing," said Heywood, "is an ornament to the city, which strangers of all nations repairing hither report of in their countries, beholding them here with some admiration." [87] Fortunately some of the reports survive, and to travelers like Kiechel of Ulm, De Witt of Utrecht, Platter of Basle, Busino of Venice, and Paul Hentzner we owe our most re-

[86] *Stage-Players Complaint* (1641), in Hazlitt, ed., *English Drama and Stage*, pp. 256-57.
[87] *Apology for Actors* (1612), Shakespeare Society Publications, No. III, p. 52.

vealing descriptions of the English theatres.[88] Some were men of consequence: Prince Lewis of Anhalt-Cöthen, Prince Lewis Frederick of Württemberg, and Duke Philip Julius of Stettin-Pomerania, who visited the playhouses three times during a week's stay in London in 1602. The foreign embassies also provided playhouse patrons. We hear of the French ambassador and his wife going to the Globe to see *Pericles*,[89] of the Spanish ambassador with all his train going to the Fortune and then banqueting with the players,[90] of the Venetian ambassador going to the Curtain and there behaving so much like the rude multitude that in Florentine eyes at least he was "pantalonissima." [91] The foreigners show no particular preference for the private as opposed to the public playhouses; probably the public playhouses had the more pronounced local color that would interest visitors from abroad.

Thus far I have said little about the audiences of the private playhouses as such—and for good reason: Shakespeare had little experience with them. His audience was that of the Rose, The Theatre, the Curtain, and the Globe. The King's Men began using Blackfriars as a winter house only after 1608, and even from that late date until he left London, the recorded performances of Shakespeare's plays were all at the Globe. His last play, *Henry VIII*, was cer-

[88] See Rye, *England as Seen by Foreigners, passim*; Chambers, *Elizabethan Stage, passim*; and citations in the present study.

[89] Chambers, *Elizabethan Stage*, II, 549.

[90] July 21, 1621. See *Letters of John Chamberlain*, ed. McClure, II, 391.

[91] Chambers, "Elizabethan Stage Gleanings," *Review of English Studies*, I (1925), 186. I have mentioned earlier the playhouse adventures of Ambassador Foscarini.

tainly first brought out there. Some misapprehension must lie behind a statement like the following: "While Shakespeare, unconsciously writing for all time, kept in his mind's eye the approval of lordly patrons of Blackfriars, Thomas Heywood and his kind catered to apprentices and shopkeepers who haunted the Red Bull." [92] We cannot have the thing both ways. If Heywood wrote for apprentices and shopkeepers, so also did Shakespeare; or if Shakespeare wrote for "lordly patrons," so also did Heywood. A source of confusion exists in the different types of audience vaguely perceived to have existed in or about Shakespeare's time. The matter requires clarification, and a preliminary word must be said about the "private" audiences.

As soon as the playhouses at Paul's and Blackfriars began to rival the Globe and Fortune, we hear that a man need no longer "be choakte with the stench of Garlicke" for at Paul's "Tis a good gentle Audience," [93] while at Blackfriars there are "Select, and most respected Auditours," [94] and plays can count on

> gentle presence, and the Sceans suckt up
> By calme attention of choyce audience.[95]

The playwrights later discovered that the attention was neither uniformly calm nor choice; however, at the rates charged, it continued "gentle." In the reign of James, multitudes of coaches were causing traffic congestions outside Blackfriars; and in that of Charles, traffic regulations were

---

[92] Wright, *Middle-Class Culture in Elizabethan England*, p. 18.
[93] Marston, *Jack Drum's Entertainment* (1600), Act V, Scene ii, in Wood, ed., *Plays*.
[94] Marston, Prologue, *Antonio and Mellida* (1599–1600).
[95] Marston, *Antonio's Revenge* (1599–1601), Act V, Scene vi, ed. Greg, Malone Society Reprints.

discommoding "diverse persons of great quality, especially Ladies and Gentlewomen" [96] on their way to the theatre. In 1636 the Duke of Lenox and the Lord Chamberlain were disputing over possession of a Blackfriars box. Between 1631 and 1641, Sir Humphrey Mildmay, during his sojourns in London, records fifty-seven visits to the theatres, usually Blackfriars, with his wife or in polite theatrical parties "with good Company." On one occasion, at least, "good Company" palled. "To dynner came Sr Chr: Abdy & wente to the Newe playe with my wife. J wente abroade by my selfe to worse places alone." [97] After the theatres were closed in 1642, a spokesman for the Phoenix, Salisbury Court, and Blackfriars affirmed that at these houses "none use to come but the best of the Nobility and Gentry" and disclaims with high disdain "boystrous Butchers, cutting Coblers, hard-handed Masons, and the like." [98] The gentility of the private playhouse audiences we dare not question.

But the private playhouses between 1599 and 1642 did not create this audience. They merely segregated and perhaps augmented it. It had been segregated once before in some slight degree, as evidenced by Lyly's allusions in the eighties to the advantages of "presenting our studies before Gentlemen" at Paul's,[99] and to the "woonted courtisies" of the spectators at Blackfriars.[100] It existed during the nineties but was then merged with other elements from the popula-

[96] Adams, *Shakespearean Playhouses*, p. 231.

[97] December 13, 1635. The dramatic extracts from Mildmay's journal (Harl. MS 454) appear in Bentley, "The Diary of a Caroline Theatre-goer," *Modern Philology*, XXXV (1937-38), 61-72.

[98] *Actors Remonstrance or Complaint* (1643), in Hazlitt, ed., *English Drama and Stage*, p. 261.

[99] Prologue, *Midas* (c. 1589), in Bond, ed., *Complete Works*.

[100] Prologue, *Campaspe* (c. 1584), in *ibid*. See also the Prologue to *Sapho and Phao* (c.1584), in *ibid*.

tion to form the universal audience of the public theatres. We should distinguish among three Elizabethan audiences, recognizing that various occasions and various theatres would obscure our distinction: there was the genteel audience of the private theatres; there was the plebeian audience of such theatres as the Red Bull and perhaps the Fortune after the private houses had filched the gentry away; and then there was that audience both genteel and plebeian, or neither, of the nineties and, because of its peculiar prestige, of the Globe in the early decades of the seventeenth century. It was the audience for which nearly all the great Elizabethan plays were written. It was Shakespeare's audience.

All that we can say of the composition of Shakespeare's audience, other than that it was a cross section of the London population of his day, is that youth may have predominated somewhat over age, male over female, the worldly over the pious, and, of course without the "perhaps," the receptive over the unreceptive. Although the more leisured classes would have been better represented than by their pro rata of the population, it was predominantly a working-class audience because of the great numerical superiority of the working classes in the London area and because theatrical tariffs had been designed largely for them. It was not much different from the assemblage which gathered to hear the sermons at Paul's Cross. Stephen Gosson, the one really likable antagonist of the Elizabethan stage, says with a kind of weary resignation: "Indeede I must confesse there comes to Playes of all sortes, old and young; it is hard to say that all offend"—then his higher nature triumphs—"yet I promise you, I wil sweare for none." [101]

[101] *Schoole of Abuse* (1579), ed. Arber, English Reprints, No. III, p. 60.

Things motley are bound to be judged by their more lurid patches. Shakespeare's age was easily deceived about the nature of its own audience. In 1602 men were needed for the army and playhouses were full of the "refuse sort of people." Two birds could be killed with one stone. The Privy Council ordered a sudden descent upon "plaie howses, Bowlinge Alleys and Dycinge howses" and the taking up of all "idle loose dissolute and suspected persons and such as cannot in your discrecion give a good accompte howe they doe lawfullie live notwithstandinge they goe apparelled like gentlemen." [102] The order has a sequel that has gone unrecorded by the historians of the stage. The "bawdy howses, and bowling allyes" were not molested (municipal favoritism?), but "All the playe howses were besett in one daye and very many pressed from thence." But behold! to the discomfiture of all concerned and the immediate need for redress "they did not only presse Gentlemen, and sarvingmen, but Lawyers, Clarkes, country men that had lawe cawses, aye the Quens men, knightes, and as it was credibly reported one Earle." [103] All kinds of fish in this sea!

The playwrights were sometimes insolent with the humbler patrons, but I have come upon mention of only one class wholly rejected from the audience:

> So good-night, kind gentles,
> For I hope there's never a Jew among you all.[104]

But in Shakespeare's audience there were probably also a few Jews.

[102] "Dramatic Records of the City of London: the Repertories, Journals, and Letter Books," in *Malone Society Collections*, II, Part III, 318.

[103] *Letters of Philip Gawdy*, ed. Jeayes, pp. 120–21.

[104] Concluding speech in *The First Part of Jeronimo* (1604–5), in Dodsley, *Select Collection of Old English Plays*, ed. Hazlitt, Vol. IV.

IV

BEHAVIOR

MODERN AMERICAN audiences are prodigiously well behaved; in public, at the theatre as at the dinner table, relish must wait upon refinement. We sit in decorous rows, scrupulously ignoring our neighbors, applauding generously and in cautious unison whatever is tolerable and well meant, suffering in docile silence whatever is feeble, dull, or foolish. The hiss, the catcall, and the boo profane no more the hallowed air. Whether such behavior amounts to an unwholesome supineness might be profitably debated; certainly it sets up a false standard for judging the Elizabethans.

Shakespeare's audience did not behave so well. Nevertheless, the boisterousness at the Globe has been overestimated. Sometimes such rowdiness and riot are envisioned that the performance of the play seems an irrelevance, a pitiable intrusion, while playgoing seems a hazardous occupation uninsurable at Lloyds, if Lloyds had then existed. Reminders are necessary. Pickpockets and prostitutes in an audience do not mean an audience of pickpockets and prostitutes—there is a law of diminishing returns. What we have really to decide is whether the criminal and unruly element in the audience was large enough and active enough to create a sinister atmosphere; whether the theatres were associated in the minds of Londoners with immorality, danger, and disorder. Initially, it seems improbable. Seeing a play is, after all, one of the more meditative pursuits and, considered *in vacuo*, neither an allurement to criminals nor an incitement to crime. Plays were the only unique attraction in the theatres. Theatregoing was voluntary; theatregoing was an expense. Elsewhere in London one could mingle with crowds and perpetrate grave crimes and minor misdemeanors without paying an admission charge.

In substantiation of the statement that "intrigues and other nefarious transactions" were carried on at the theatres and that "law-court and other records preserve the memory of both grave crimes and minor misdemeanours of which they were the scenes," [1] Sir Edmund Chambers offers evidence like the following:

The Middlesex justices had to deal with cases of stealing a purse at the Curtain in 1600, of a "notable outrage" at the Red Bull in 1610, or stealing a purse at the Red Bull in 1613, and of stabbing at the Fortune in 1613 (*Middlesex County Records*, I, 205, 217, 259; II, xlvii, 64, 71, 86, 88). [2]

Recognizing though I do that the the above forms only a part of Chambers's list of offenses and that the effect of such a list is cumulative, I still submit it as my judgment that

[1] See p. 5.
[2] Chambers, *Elizabethan Stage*, I, 264, note 5. Citation of these crimes at the Fortune is repeated in *ibid.*, II, 441.

"so far as the external abuses of theatres go, the complaints of their bitterest enemies" are not "fairly well supported by independent evidence." [3] That legal offenses were committed at the theatres is in no need of proof—it might be taken for granted. That such offenses were committed at the theatres commonly, more commonly there than elsewhere, has not been proved.

We must remember two things: first, that the justices were allied in interest with those who denounced the theatres in general terms and were solicitous that every playhouse offense should be a *cause célèbre*; and, second, that court records by their very nature are memorials of the abnormal and apt to warp the view. In the law-abiding communities where most of us live, crimes are committed every day. Shakespeare and his theatre have been objects of such keen interest that court records have been ransacked. Cause for reflection is given us by the editor's preface to those same *Middlesex County Records* of which Chambers makes use:

XIV. Choice of Documents.—It will be for the reader's satisfaction that I should indicate the various considerations that have determined my choice of documents for especial notice in the ensuing calendar. Throughout my labours I have been controlled by the opinion that I ought to call attention to those writings, which afford particulars, however minute, of new or otherwise peculiar information, likely to be in any way or degree serviceable to historians, biographers, students in any department of literary research, or artists in form and colour.[4]

Obviously, by the modern recorder as by the Elizabethan, although from a purer motive, playhouse crimes are not to be missed.

[3] See p. 5.   [4] *Middlesex County Records*, ed. Jeaffreson, I, xlix.

At least some attempt at statistical method should precede generalization. In the limited degree to which statistical method is possible in the present case, it argues for the law-abiding nature of Elizabethan audiences. If it is fair to remark that the Middlesex justices dealt with a crime at the Curtain in 1600, it is also fair to add that they dealt, so far as we know, with only one, whereas there were hundreds of acting days in the year with throngs of spectators in at-tendance each day. If we hear of a second crime in 1610, we should pause in breathless admiration at the stainless interval from 1600 to 1610. The least we can do is to view playhouse disorders against the general background. In 1600 a recognizance was taken for the cutting of a purse at the Curtain. If a true bill were found, this would be a capital felony. In the year 1600 the Middlesex justices must have taken many recognizances because 118 true bills were found, all for offenses committed elsewhere than in play-houses.[5] In 1610 a purse was cut at the Red Bull. In this year, in the jurisdiction of the Middlesex justices, true bills were found for 15 larcenies from the person besides 47 other larcenies (none committed in playhouses), not to mention housebreakings, burglaries, and horse-stealings.[6] In 1613 there was a stabbing at the Fortune, but elsewhere than at the Fortune there were 11 murders, 12 cases of man-slaughter, 28 cases of assault and battery, 3 assaults with a sword, and 7 attacks upon officers. Seventy-two males and four females were sentenced to be hanged.[7] Evidently the playhouses were relatively safe.

The centers of criminality in Elizabethan London were not the playhouses but, as we might expect, the alehouses

[5] *Ibid.*, II, 282.   [6] *Ibid.*, p. 296.   [7] *Ibid.*, p. 297–98.

and taverns.[8] Such crimes as were committed at plays were
the concomitant of crowds and bear no relation to theatres
as such or to the mood of audiences or the type of people
composing them. Wherever there were crowds there were
pickpockets: "their gains lies by all places of resort and assemblies, therefore their chief walks is Paul's, Westminster,
the Exchange, plays, bear-garden, running at tilt, the Lord
Mayor's day, and festival meetings, frays, shootings, or great
fairs." [9] In the favor of pickpockets, the plays, we observe,
share place with the Exchange, Paul's, and Westminster—
the centers respectively of commerce, religion, and the
law. In Dekker's *The Bel-Man of London,* churches, mar-
kets, and law courts are revealed to have been as popular
with the fraternity as the theatres, while the parade of civic
virtues in the Lord Mayor's pageants furnished a field day
for the vicious.[10]

The number of prostitutes who attended the theatres and
the amount of solicitation carried on there cannot now be
determined. From the very nature of the case some doubt
in the matter must have existed among the more scientific
minds of Shakespeare's own day. However, a calm con-
templation of the problem of sin, especially sexual sin, is
not to be looked for among those who share that attitude
of mind which we term puritanical: Elizabethan censors
were prone to believe the worst. Encouragement to evil-
thinking resided in the fact that the theatres did actually
bring men and women informally together, in a sociable and
even flirtatious mood. At a country performance we hear

[8] Judges, ed., *Elizabethan Underworld, passim.*
[9] Greene, *Second and Last Part of Connycatching* (1591), in *ibid.,*
p. 162.
[10] In Grosart, ed., *Non-Dramatic Works,* III, 157–59.

that "The people which were in the Roome were exceeding Joviall, and merry before the Play began, Young men and Maides dancing together, and so merry and frolick were many of the Spectators, that the Players could hardly get Liberty that they themselves might Act." [11]

London audiences would have been less buoyant—but not repressed. Gosson and Stubbes provide us with an interesting sequence. First, the arrivals:

In the playhouses at London, it is the fashion of youthes to go first into the yarde, and to carry theire eye through euery gallery, then like vnto rauens where they spye the carion thither they flye, and presse as nere to ye fairest as they can.[12]

Then the assembled audience:

you shall see suche heauing, and shoouing, suche ytching and shouldring, too sitte by women; Suche care for their garments, that they bee not trode on: Such eyes to their lappes, that no chippes light in them: Such pillowes to ther backes, that they take no hurte: Such masking in their eares, I knowe not what: Such giuing them Pippins to passe the time: Suche playing at foote Saunt without Cardes: Such ticking, such toying, such smiling, such winking . . . that it is a right Comedie.[13]

And finally the departures:

Than, these goodly pageants being done, euery mate sorts to his mate, euery one bringes another homeward of their way verye freendly, and in their secret conclaues (couertly) they play the Sodomits, or worse.[14]

---

[11] John Rowe, *Tragi-Comoedia: Being a Brief Relation of the Strange, and Wonderfull Hand of God Discovered at Witney* (1653), signature ✳.

[12] Gosson, *Playes Confuted in Fiue Actions* (1582), in Hazlitt, ed., *English Drama and Stage*, p. 215.

[13] Gosson, *Schoole of Abuse* (1579), ed. Arber, English Reprints, No. III, p. 35.

[14] Stubbes, *Anatomie of Abuses* (1583), ed. Furnivall, New Shakspere Society Publications, Ser. VI, No. VI, p. 145.

Observe in the last line where description ends and conjecture begins.

To an observer like Thomas Nashe, playhouse flirtation seemed not only innocent but educational. In a pamphlet which sincerely flagellates lechery, Nashe approves of the young gallant who

haunts Plaies, & sharpens his wits with frequenting the company of Poets: he emboldens his blushing face by courting faire women on the sodaine, and lookes into all Estates by conuersing with them in publike places.[15]

But beauty is in the eye of the beholder; compare with the following:

Whosoeuer shal visit the chappel of Satan, I meane the Theater, shal finde there no want of yong ruffins, nor lacke of harlots, vtterlie past al shame: who presse to the fore-frunt of the scaffoldes, to the end to showe their impudencie, and to be an obiect to al mens eies. Yea, such is their open shameles behauior, as euerie man maie perceaue by their wanton gestures, wherevnto they are giuen; yea, they seeme there to be like brothels of the stewes. For often without respect of the place, and company which behold them, they commit that filthines openlie, which is horrible to be done in secret; as if whatsoeuer they did, were warranted.[16]

That the writer, in his enthusiasm, is applying the word "filthiness" to what is now called "petting" is apparent from an admission by a member of his own party, who used the term in the more usual sense. "Not that any filthynesse in deede," said Gosson, "is committed within the compasse of that grounde";[17] the bitterest critics of the theatres stop

---

[15] *Pierce Penilesse, His Supplication to the Divell* (1592), in McKerrow, ed., *Works*, I, 210.

[16] *Second and Third Blast of Retrait from Plaies and Theaters* (1580), in Hazlitt, ed., *English Drama and Stage*, p. 139.

[17] *Schoole of Abuse* (1579), ed. Arber, English Reprints, No. III, p. 35.

with the charge that they are the scene of "privy and un-mete contracts." A modern writer seems to go further. Commenting on Dekker's statement that the lords' room "by the iniquity of custome, conspiracy of waiting women and Gentle-men-Ushers, are contemptibly thrust into the reare, and much new Satten is there dambd, by being smothred to death in darknesse," W. J. Lawrence says that since the lords' room is called the "stages Suburbs" and since "Suburbs" must have been used in "a sinister metaphorical sense," the cupidity of the players had induced them to turn the lords' room into "a licentious rendezvous for the lower middle classes." [18] But my dear Sir!

The English courtesan was not, as in several continental nations, distinguishable by her attire. Thomas Cranley's *Amanda,* although belonging to 1635, describes a practice that probably prevailed throughout our period:

> Like to a chamber-maid thou com'st to-day:
> The next day after thou dost change thy note;
> Then like a country wench thou com'st in grey,
> And sittest like a stranger at the play:
>   Tomorrow after that, thou comest then
>   In the neat habit of a citizen.
> The next time rushing in thy silken weeds
> Embroider'd, lac'd, perfum'd, in glittering show;
> So that thy look an admiration breeds,
> Rich like a lady and attended so:
> As brave as any countess dost thou go.[19]

It is in the last of the above metamorphoses that we have our most detailed picture of a courtesan in an Elizabethan play-

[18] *Elizabethan Playhouse and Other Studies,* I, 30–31.
[19] Quoted in Collier, *History of English Dramatic Poetry,* III, 411.

house. Chaplain Busino of the Venetian embassy was accosted during a visit to the Fortune in 1617–18:

Scarcely was I seated ere a very elegant dame, but in a mask, came and placed herself beside me. . . . She asked me for my address both in French and English; and, on my turning a deaf ear, she determined to honour me by showing me some fine diamonds on her fingers, repeatedly taking off no fewer than three gloves, which were worn one over the other. . . . This lady's bodice was of yellow satin richly embroidered, her petticoat of gold tissue with stripes, her robe of red velvet with a raised pile, lined with yellow muslin with broad stripes of pure gold. She wore an apron of point lace of various patterns: her head-tire was highly perfumed, and the collar of white satin beneath the delicately-wrought ruff struck me as extremely pretty.[20]

That this "elegant dame" was a courtesan seems likely, although Busino does not say so and it is impossible to know. If so, she was literally a bona roba such as would have added "tone" to the gathering. If courtesans assumed the attire of chambermaids and ladies, the neat habits of citizens and of country wenches in grey, they must have had a regard for the proprieties. We cannot take too seriously the tendency of the Elizabethan satirist to identify as a "punk" any young woman seen conversing with a man.[21] An amusing contradiction exists in the writings of those who called the theatres "An appointed place for Bauderie," for whereas they imply that all the women in the audience are abandoned, they also

[20] "Diaries and Despatches of the Venetian Embassy at the Court of King James I, in the Years 1617, 1618," *Quarterly Review*, CII (1857), 416.

[21] See Dekker, *Newes from Hell* (1606), *Iests to Make you Merrie* (1607), and *Lanthorne and Candle-Light* (1609), in Grosart, ed., *Non-Dramatic Works*, II, 96, 292; III, 269.

insist that "the most honest wife is the soonest assalted" [22] and seem quite concerned for the virtue of women who presumably have none to lose. We may safely conclude that solicitation in the playhouses would have been no more open than in London assemblies generally and that the disinterested spectator would have been either unconscious of it or accustomed to it. There is a great deal of justice in a retrospective defense of the theatres written after they were closed:

> though some have taxed our Houses unjustly for being the receptacles of Harlots, the exchanges where they meet and make their bargaines with their franck chapmen of the Country and City, yet we may justly excuse our selves of either knowledge or consent in these lewd practices, we having no propheticke soules to know womens honesty by instinct, nor commission to examine them.[23]

The afflictions most commonly associated with Elizabethan audiences are frays and riotousness. Two friends of the stage may be permitted to testify first:

> Whereas some Petitioners of the Counsaile against them obiect, they corrupt the youth of the Cittie, and withdrawe Prentises from theyr worke; they heartily wishe they might bee troubled with none of their youth nor their prentises; for some of them (I meane the ruder handicrafts seruants) neuer come abroade, but they are in danger of vndoing: and as for corrupting them when they come, thats false; for no Play they haue, encourageth any man to tumults or rebellion, but layes before such the halter and the gallowes.[24]

---

[22] *Second and Third Blast of Retrait from Plaies and Theaters* (1580), in Hazlitt, ed., *English Drama and Stage*, pp. 125–26.

[23] *Actors Remonstrance or Complaint* (1643), in Hazlitt, ed., *English Drama and Stage*, pp. 261–62.

[24] *Pierce Penilesse, His Supplication to the Divell* (1592), in McKerrow, ed., *Works*, I, 213–14.

Nashe's sentiments are echoed by Henry Chettle:

> And lette [the ghost of] Tarleton intreate the yoong people of the Cittie, either to abstaine altogether from playes, or at their comming thither to vse themselues after a more quiet order.
>
> In a place so ciuill as this Cittie is esteemed, it is more than barbarously rude, to see the shamefull disorder and routes that sometime in such publike meetings are vsed.
>
> The beginners are neither gentlemen, nor citizens, nor any of both their seruants, but some lewd mates that long for innouation; & when they see aduantage, that either Seruingmen or Apprentises are most in number, they will be of either side, though indeed they are of no side, but men beside all honestie, willing to make boote of cloakes, hats, purses, or what euer they can lay holde on in a hurley burley. These are the common causers of discord in publike places. If otherwise it happen (as it seldome doth) that any quarrell be betweene man and man, it is far from manhood to make so publike a place their field to fight in: no men will doe it, but cowardes that would faine be parted, or haue hope to haue manie partakers.[25]

Chettle here affirms that personal quarrels are infrequent in the theatres, but he deplores with Nashe a type of disorder fresh in the minds of both because it had resulted in the closing down of the theatres shortly before their pamphlets were written.

The situation was as follows. Between the apprentices (who felt that London was theirs) and the young gentlemen placed out in service (who were insistent upon their social superiority) there existed a natural antagonism. At places where these factions met in numbers, trouble was

[25] *Kind-Harts Dreame* (1592), in Ingleby, ed., *Shakspere Allusion-Books*, New Shakspere Society Publications, Ser. IV, No. 1, Part I, pp. 65–66.

apt to brew, especially in the presence of setters-on who would profit by a melee. Chettle is an accurate observer, and a case of precisely the sort of thing he had in mind occurred in June of 1584. William Fleetwood, Recorder of London, reported that "nere the Theatre or Curten at the tyme of the Playes there laye a prentice sleeping vpon the Grasse and one Challes at Grostock dyd turne vpon the too vpon the belly of the same prentice." [26] Understandably, a fight ensued, and Challes with his mates, who "were litell better than roogs that took vpon theym the name of gentilmen," proclaimed that "prentizes were but the skomme of the worlde." On the following days the apprentices, already in a mood for "mutines and assembles," were whipped on by one Browne, "a shifting fellowe having a perrelous witt of his owne entending a spoil if he cold have brought it to passe." Browne's methods lacked subtlety: he bullied "certen poor boyes handicraft prentises" standing at the door of The Theatre and wounded one of them in the hand. Crowds milled about, the growing ill-feeling creating disturbances in various parts of London. Fleetwood's underlying sympathies must have been with the apprentices—a note of pride creeps into his report of the next episode: "my lo ffitzgerrold with a nosmber of gentilmen with hym at moor gatt met a tall yong fellowe being a pretize and strooke hym vpon the face with his hatt wherevpon my lo and his compane were glad to take a howse." All of this, be it noted, has to do with the theatres only in that it began in the fields nearby, where the belly of the sleeping apprentice tempted the toe

[26] "Dramatic Records from the Lansdowne Manuscripts," in *Malone Society Collections*, I, Part II, 164–66.

of a shoddy young gentleman. The logical conclusion of the Lord Mayor and Aldermen was that The Theatre and Curtain should be pulled down.

In June, 1592, a feud flared up between the fellmongers of Southwark and the officers of the knight marshal. The officers had a warrant to serve upon a workman and, according to the depositions in the case, "entred the house, whear the warrant was to bee served with a dagger drawen affreyting the goodwyfe who satt by the fire with a young infant in hir armes." A touching scene! with the sanctity of hearth-side and motherhood violated. The fellmongers must be avenged! Unfortunately for the drama, in attempting to rescue the arrested workman from the Marshalsea, the crusaders "assembled themselues by occasion, & pretence of their meeting at a play, which bysides the breach of ye Sabboth day giveth opportunitie of committing these & such lyke disorders." [27] The theatres in consequence were closed from June 23 to the following Michaelmas.

The disturbances just described are the only ones of the kind recorded in any detail; in both cases the theatres seem to have functioned as scapegoats. Chambers speaks of a document of 1595, wherein "the origin of yet another prentice riot was traced to the obnoxious performances." [28] But the document in question reads that plays and theatres

wee verely think to bee the cheif cause, aswell of many other disorders & lewd demeanours which appear of late in young people of all degrees, as of the late stirr & mutinous attempt of those fiew apprentices and other seruantes, who wee doubt not driew their infection from these & like places. [29]

[27] *Ibid.*, p. 188. [28] *Elizabethan Stage*, I, 297.
[29] "Dramatic Records of the City of London: the Remembrancia," in *Malone Society Collections*, I, Part I, 76.

The traces are pretty faint, existing it appears chiefly in the interpretive minds of the civic officials. We can take no more seriously a similar document of 1597, in which certain unspecified culprits arrested for unspecified crimes are alleged to have said that the theatres were the meeting place for their "mutinous attempts." [30]

It is little wonder that the Lord Mayor and aldermen made all that they could of even the slenderest relationship between theatres and riots. They could be certain that, in this matter at least, the Privy Council, ever on the alert for rebellions, would lend an attentive ear. Assemblies were dangerous, and audiences were assemblies: here was solid ground. But after 1592 the enemy failed them, and in the absence of anything definite the city fathers resorted to vague mutterings and reminders. They have little meaning. Real disorders would have resulted in specific charges and in real penalties. The evidence for habitual riotousness in Shakespeare's audience becomes tenuous upon examination. It resembles the evidence for rebelliousness in Elizabethan England generally. The popular uprisings of the time seem pathetically feeble and inadequate in view of the seriousness with which they were taken and the cruelty with which they were suppressed. If our two instances of riots about the theatres prove anything, they prove, in their denouements, that audiences were normally peaceful; otherwise the theatres would have been clamped permanently shut.

On one score the Elizabethan audience comes off better than would any modern audience under similar circumstances. Three disasters occurred in the theatres with the spectators assembled. Each is described by an inimical writer,

[30] *Ibid.*, p. 78.

yet in no case is there evidence of panic. On April 6, 1580, an earthquake rocked The Theatre and the Curtain. Stubbes writes of the spectators maiming themselves by leaping from "the turrets, pinacles, and towres, wher they stood," [31] but the fact appears to be that the only casualties of the day were two children attending a sermon in Christ Church.[32] On January 13, 1583, the galleries of the Bear Garden collapsed. With a terrible zest, Stubbes describes how seven spectators were "killed dead," some with their "heads all to squasht," [33] but the injuries appear to have been the result of the collapse itself. The spectators extricated each other and bore the injured home. On June 29, 1613, the Globe burned to the ground in a single hour, "and yt was a great marvayle and fayre grace of God, that the people had so litle harme, having but two narrow doores to get out." [34] It was a fair grace of God manifested in the self-control of Shakespeare's audience. The theatre was a death-trap, filled to capacity for the spectacular first performance of *Henry VIII*.

No "frays" originating actually within the theatres are on record for Shakespeare's own period, but there are two earlier examples. In April, 1580, there was "a certaine fraye betwene the servauntes of th'erle of Oxforde and the gentle-men of the Innes of the Courtes." [35] We cannot expect much impartiality among the authorities when law students come

---

[31] *Anatomie of Abuses* (1583), ed. Furnivall, New Shakspere Society Publications, Ser. VI, No. VI, p. 180.

[32] Chambers, *Elizabethan Stage*, IV, 208.

[33] *Anatomie of Abuses* (1583), ed. Furnivall, New Shakspere Society Publications, Ser. VI, No. VI, p. 179.

[34] *Letters of John Chamberlain*, ed. McClure, I, 467.

[35] Minutes of the Privy Council, April–July, 1580, quoted in Chambers, *Elizabethan Stage*, IV, 280.

in conflict with such "superfluous sort of men" as actors, and
we are not surprised to hear of two of the actors being sent
to Marshalsea "for committing of disorders and frayes appon
the gentlemen of the Innes of the Courte." [36] In July, 1581,
there was a similar quarrel between the Gentlemen of Gray's
Inn and some of Lord Berkeley's Men.[37] No detailed information about these conflicts survives, not enough even to
prove that they originated in the theatres, although they
probably did; but if similar records were plentiful, we
might justly conclude that a potential enmity existed between actors and audience. Such records, however, begin
and end with these two early examples.

Theatres were sometimes molested as part of the Shrove
Tuesday bacchanalia of the apprentices, once quite seriously
in 1617 when the new Phoenix was badly damaged; but
these outbursts have no especial significance in dramatic
history. Theatres, brothels, and similar places—conspicuous and public—attracted revelers in a suggestible mood.
Churches and citizens' houses were naturally immune, and
something had to be destroyed. Riotous collegians now de-
trolley street cars and destroy goal posts, expressing thus
no general pique against public transit or the game of football. Only twice are we confronted with Elizabethan audiences in a vengeful mood, and each time the provocation
was great. Having paid premium prices, the spectators were
defrauded of their entertainment. In 1614 at the Hope,
after John Taylor had advertised a contest of extemporal
wit, his rival failed to appear.[38] In 1602 Richard Vennor,
having promised a magnificent operatic display to be per-

[36] *Ibid.*   [37] *Ibid.*, p. 282.
[38] Adams, *Shakespearean Playhouses*, p. 333.

formed by gentlemen and gentlewomen at the Swan, ex-
acted eighteenpence and two-shilling admission charges and
then decamped with the proceeds—whereupon "the common
people when they saw themselves deluded, revenged themselves upon the hangings, curtaines, stooles, walles, and
whatsoever came in theyre way very outragiously and made
great spoyle: there was great store of good companie and
many noble men." [39] The ingenuous reader will confess that
in the circumstances he might have gone into action himself; such episodes belong to no one age and obliterate the
distinctions between "common people" and "good companie."

The onepenny patrons are apt to be particular sufferers
from our preconceptions of Elizabethan theatrical behavior.
W. J. Lawrence writes that "Attendants must have been
placed at frequent intervals to keep each portion of the audience in its place during the performance, otherwise the
Groundlings would have been unceasing in their invasion
of the higher regions." [40] As doors have locks, so the lower
gallery of Elizabethan theatres had spiked railings; otherwise there is no evidence whatever for Lawrence's supposi-
tion. The acting companies seem to have got along admirably
without the aid of civil officers within the houses, and we
hear of no employee functioning as "bouncer." The gatherers were sometimes, in fact, elderly widows holding their
positions as a company obligation. A disposition to interrupt
the performance, by the Gentlemen in Day's *Isle of Gulls*
and by the Grocer's family in Beaumont's *Knight of the
Burning Pestle*, is combated by the child actors with appeals

[39] *Letters of John Chamberlain*, ed. McClure, I, 172.
[40] *Elizabethan Playhouse and Other Studies*, II, 98.

for coöperation or capitulation to the demands. The adult actors were able men, but without power over an audience unless it was self-policed. A hint of such policing occurs in Dekker's *Guls Horne-Booke* (1609), and it comes from the groundlings. Twice while the gallant is making a nuisance of himself comes the cry "Away with the fool!"—once from the "rabble" and again from "all the garlike-mouthed stink-ards." [41]

The gentry were no paragons of deportment. At court banquets following masks, the food was apt to be so "rapa-ciously swept away" as to send the tables crashing; and when the Knights of the Bath were entertained by the Lord Mayor at Drapers Hall in 1616, "some of them were so rude and unruly and caried themselves so insolently divers wayes but specially in putting citizens wives to the squeake" [42] that the party broke up without the serving of the dinner. Jonson's bitterest complaints are not at groundlings but at "caprichious gallants" such as "haue taken such a habit of dislike in all things, that they will approue nothing, be it neuer so con-ceited or elaborate, but sit disperst, making faces, and spit-ting, wagging their vpright eares, and cry filthy, filthy." [43] Dekker's Gull does not confine himself to a display of ennui; he exhausts human ingenuity in becoming an active pest: he arrives late, sits on the stage, laughs aloud during tragic scenes, tickles the ear of his neighbor with a straw, and makes a noisy exit at the climax of the play. Showing off on such a scale could not have been common even among capricious gallants; indeed Dekker himself clearly implies

---

[41] In Grosart, ed., *Non-Dramatic Works*, II, 203, 250.
[42] *Letters of John Chamberlain*, ed. McClure, II, 34.
[43] *The Case Is Altered* (before 1609), Act II, Scene vii, in Herford and Simpson, eds., *Ben Jonson*.

that to tarry too long before the anger of the "opposed rascality" was not safe. It is probable that both the upper and lower classes behaved best when each was under the surveillance of the other, before the audience was split in two by the system of high-priced and low-priced theatres. It is to the post-Shakespearean years that the complaints, never very numerous, about bad conduct in the audience mostly belong. It is then that plebeian audiences interrupted the players to demand the performance of old favorites instead of the play originally billed [44] and that the gallants in the private theatres displayed the contempt that enraged Ben Jonson. Yet even the audiences of these years were looked back upon as models of decorum in Restoration times.[45]

Considerable good feeling evidently existed between the acting companies and the public. We must not be deceived by the manner in which officialdom clung to the antique terms classifying actors as masterless men and vagabonds. Actors "walked gentlemen," and their prestige was great with the rank and file. An appropriate symbolism exists in the Elizabethan playhouse with its stage in the heart of the audience. The great actors like Tarleton, Alleyn, Burbage, and Kempe were respected and loved. Young gentlemen became hero-worshipers. Among the reforms claimed for the Caroline theatre was:

[44] Edmund Gayton, *Festivous Notes on Don Quixote* (1654), quoted in Collier, *History of English Dramatic Poetry*, III, 417. See also Chambers, "Elizabethan Stage Gleanings," *Review of English Studies*, I (1925), 186.

[45] James Wright, *Historia Histrionica* (1699), in Dodsley, *Select Collection of Old English Plays*, ed. Hazlitt, Vol. XV: "Then the prices were small (there being no scenes), and better order kept among the company that came."

the inveigling in young Gentlemen, Merchants Factors, and Prentizes to spend their patrimonies and Masters estates upon us and our Harlots in Tavernes [has ceased]; we have cleane and quite given over the borrowing money at first sight of punie gallants or praising their swords, belts and beavers, so to invite them to bestow them upon us.[46]

We cannot take too literally a statement like the following of 1638, but there is no evidence to refute it:

> they, he swears, to th' Theatre would come
> Ere they had din'd to take up the best room;
> Then sit on benches, not adorn'd with mats
> And graciously did vail their high-crowned hats
> To every half dress'd Player, as he still
> Through th' hangings peep'd to see how th' house did fill.[47]

A tendency to visit the sins of the children upon the parents has existed in stage chronicles, to note the behavior in theatres in the mid-eighteenth century and to conclude that if audiences could be thus one hundred and fifty years ago, then three hundred years ago they must have been twice as bad. But new times generate new abuses, and, for certain abuses of the Restoration and later theatres, there is no evidence whatever in the Elizabethan. The actors apparently were not pilloried for personal or political reasons, and the companies were not forced to view their forestage as a first line of defense against an embattled multitude.

If Shakespeare's audience was noisy before the play, silence prevailed when the play began. Prologues occasionally prayed for silence just as epilogues prayed for ap-

[46] *Actors Remonstrance or Complaint*, in Hazlitt, ed., *English Drama and Stage*, pp. 260–61.
[47] Davenant, Prologue, *The Unfortunate Lovers* (1638), in Maidment and Logan, eds., *Dramatic Works*.

plause.[48] The only complaints that occur in number about disturbing sounds during performances refer to nutcracking.[49] If such sounds as this could provide the major annoyance (like coughing and paper-rustling now), a standard of silence may be inferred little inferior to ours. C. J. Sisson has remarked with unimpeachable logic: "Il n'est donc pas inutile de redire que les pièces de Shakespeare ont été écrites pour l'auditorie du Globe . . . et que le populaire y'a payé le prix d'entrée pour les écouter et non pour se refuser à les écouter." [50] What indeed would have been the point of noisiness and inattention? The spectators who could afford to do so smoked during the performance and drank bottled ale during the intermissions. These ministrations to the body argue no deficiency of soul.

The satirical pamphleteers of Shakespeare's day have a buoyant and witty style. They hold no steel glass up to nature. Consider the following:

What swearing is there, yea, what swaggering, what facing and out-facing? what shuffling, what shouldering, what Iustling, what Ieering, what byting of Thumbs to beget quarrels, what holding vppe of fingers to remember drunken meetings, what brauing with Feathers, what bearding with Mustachios, what casting open of cloakes to publish new clothes, what muffling in cloakes to hyde broken Elbows.[51]

---

[48] See the prologues to *Alarum for London* (c.1599); *Merry Devil of Edmonton* (c.1602); and *Whore of Babylon* (c.1606).

[49] Collected in W. J. Lawrence, *Those Nut-Cracking Elizabethans*, pp. 1-9.

[50] *Le Goût public et le théâtre élisabéthain*, pp. 52-53. The author has also pointed out (pp. 53-54) that a sympathetic hearing is given to poetic drama in modern English theatres where Elizabethan manners are paralleled: "Les galeries sont bruyantes encore, mais le silence descend devant le génie de l'actrice à la voix d'or, devant les beaux vers et les belles émotions d'une tragédie lointaine."

[51] Dekker, *The Dead Tearme* (1608), in Grosart, ed., *Non-Dramatic Works*, IV, 50-51.

This, as it happens, is a description not of a playhouse audience but of Londoners strolling in the walks of St. Paul's Cathedral. The playhouses stimulated the author to even more colorful efforts, and his junketing Gull has sometimes been taken to exemplify typical audience behavior. Not a single one of the foreign visitors, who have given us our most objective and trustworthy view of the Elizabethan theatre, has anything to say about disorder in the audience. On the contrary, "the best treat was to see such a crowd of nobility so very well arrayed that they looked like so many princes listening as silently and soberly as possible." [52] The playhouse was only the Fortune, but to Busino the audience seemed "a crowd of nobility." If his eyes descended to the pit, he must have seen nothing to deface the picture.

Shakespeare's audience gathered to enjoy an experience dearly bought with time and money. They wore their finest clothes.

For few of either sex come thither, but in theyr holy-dayes appareil, and so set forth, so trimmed, so adorned, so decked, so perfumed, as if they made the place the market of wantonnesse, and by consequence to unfit for a Priest to frequent. [53]

They enjoyed the opportunity to mingle with each other, and some of the men and women who had come singly flirted and made friends. The atmosphere was gay. But they had come to see a play, and the criminal or quarrelsome or persistently noisy were a threat to their enjoyment. Usually

[52] "Diaries and Despatches of the Venetian Embassy at the Court of King James I, in the Years 1617, 1618," *Quarterly Review*, CII (1857), 416.

[53] Prohibition of William Harison, Archpriest, wherein English secular priests are forbidden to attend the theatres, March 9, 1617, f.25r. Manuscript in the Folger Shakespeare Library.

their enjoyment was unimpaired. A pleasing passage inspired by the audience of the Fortune gives us an idea of what Shakespeare saw in the Globe when *As You Like It* was performed and he peered outward through the misty eyes of old Adam:

> Nay, when you look into my galleries,
> How bravely they're trimmed up, you all shall swear
> You're highly pleas'd to see what's set down there:
> Stories of men and women, mix'd together,
> Fair ones with foul, like sunshine in wet weather;
> Within one square a thousand heads are laid,
> So close that all of heads the room seems made;
> As many faces there, fill'd with blithe looks
> Shew like the promising titles of new books
> Writ merrily, the readers being their own eyes,
> Which seem to move and to give plaudities;
> And here and there, whilst with obsequious ears
> Throng'd heaps do listen, a cut-purse thrusts and leers
> With hawk's eyes for his prey; I need not shew him;
> By a hanging, villainous look yourselves may know him,
> The face is drawn so rarely: then, sir, below,
> The very floor, as 't were, waves to and fro,
> And, like a floating island, seems to move
> Upon a sea bound in with shores above.
> ALL.   These sights are excellent! [54]

Little has been said thus far of the behavior of the audience as an audience—of the visible signs of its attitude toward the plays. The general topic of responsiveness will be treated in the following chapter, but a word about its external manifestations may be added here. The poet could

---

[54] *The Roaring Girl* (1604–10), Act I, Scene i. Quoted in Adams, *Shakespearean Playhouses*, p. 279. The audience is similarly pointed out, though more briefly, in the Epilogue to *Eastward Hoe* (1605).

read the fate of his play in the faces of the multitude. If fortunate, he could

> giue an Actor, Sorrow, Rage, Ioy, Passion,
> Whilst hee againe (by selfe-same Agitation)
> Commands the Hearers, sometimes drawing out Teares,
> Then Smiles, and fills them both with Hopes & Feares.[55]

Notwithstanding the huge mixed company and the day-lighted theatres, spectators literally wept. Nashe speaks of the "teares of ten thousand spectators" evoked by the fate of brave Talbot,[56] and such allusions are not uncommon. When a bit of comedy struck home, the audience laughed in mighty volume: "in the Theaters they generally take vp a wonderfull laughter, and shout altogether with one voyce, when they see some notable cosenedge practised." [57] Concerning the general opinion upon their offering the actors were never kept in doubt. No mechanical aids to noisemaking appear to have been utilized by the audience, as in the eighteenth century, but if the play failed to please, it was uncompromisingly mewed and hissed. No worse affliction for playwrights could occur to their enemies:

> When they haue writ a sceene in which their brains
> Haue dropt there deerest sweetes, and their swoln vains
> Emptied their Cundits of their purest spirit;
> As they stand gaping to recieue their merrit,
> Instead of plaudits, their chiefest blisses,
> Let their desarts be crowned with mewes and hisses.[58]

---

[55] Dekker, Prologue, *If It Be Not Good the Devil Is in It* (1610–12), in Shepherd, ed., *Dramatic Works.*

[56] See p. 49.

[57] Gosson, *Playes Confuted in Fiue Actions* (1582), in Hazlitt, ed., *English Drama and Stage*, p. 184.

[58] Day, *Isle of Gulls* (1606), Act IV, Scene iv, in Bullen, ed., *Works.*

But applause, expressed by hand clapping and cries of approval, was correspondingly hearty. "Player is much out of countenance, if fooles doe not laugh at them, boyes clappe their hands, pesants ope their throates, and the rude raskal rabble cry excellent, excellent." [59] "Excellent" is a fine word on the lips of a rabble. That Elizabethan applause was loud and enthusiastic is affirmed by many an angry moralist and many a sneering aspirant whose dramatic offering had failed to evoke it. Whatever may be said of the crimes and misdemeanors of Shakespeare's audience, it was never guilty of that final affront to art and artists—an attitude of apathy and indifference.

[59] T. G.[ainsford?], *The Rich Cabinet Furnished with Varietie of Descriptions* (1616), in Hazlitt, ed., *English Drama and Stage*, p. 230.

V

QUALITY: ELIZABETHAN
APPRAISALS

SHAKESPEARE was not confronted with cold spectators. "Comedyes make our delight exceede, for at them many times we laugh so extreemely, that striving to bridle our selues, wee cannot," writes Gosson, "delight beeing moued with varietie of shewes, of euentes, of musicke, the longer we gaze, the more we craue, yea so forcible they are, that afterwards being but thought vpon, they make vs seeke for the like an other time." And despite all those evils "dayly revealed by learned Preachers," he sighs at last, "yet will not my countrymen leaue their Playes, because Playes are the nowrishers of delight." [1] Whatever taunts were hurled at players and playmakers, ineffectuality was not one of them:

Furthermore, a man is not wearied . . . because they doo not onely (as I say) feed the eare with sweete words, equally ballanced, the eye with variable delight, but also with great allacritie doth swiftly runne ouer in two hours space, the dooings of

---

[1] *Playes Confuted in Fiue Actions* (1582), in Hazlitt, ed., *English Drama and Stage*, pp. 206, 211.

many yeares, galloping from one countrey to an other, whereby the minde is drawne into expectation of the sequell, and carried from one thing to an other with changeable motions, that although hee were vnacquainted with the matter before, yet the cunning Art hee seeth in the conueyance, maketh him patiently attend the Catastrophae: when as at a Lecture and holy exercise, all the sences are mortified and possest with drowsinesse.[2]

Always we are made aware that not only the chance to laugh and to watch the tale unfold delighted the spectators but also the "sweete words, equally ballanced," the melody of song and of speech. Tragedy was welcome provided the poetry was there to save it from "Killing the Hearers hearts":

> Give me That Man,
> Who when the Plague of an Impostumd Braynes
> (Breaking out) infects a Theatre, and hotly raignes,
> Killing the Hearers hearts, that the vast roomes
> Stand empty, like so many Dead-mens toombes,
> Can call the Banishd Auditor home, And tye
> His Eare (with golden chaines) to his Melody:[3]

The emotional susceptibility of the audience was part of the grounds of complaint against the theatres: "taking pittie on the deceitful teares of the stage louers" has vanquished the chastity of many women:

The wilines and craft of the stage is not yet so great, as is without on the scaffoldes. For that they which are euil disposed, no sooner heare anie thing spoken that maie serue their turne, but they applie it vnto them selues. Alas, saie they to their familiar by them, Gentlewoman, is it not pittie this passioned louer should

---

[2] Crosse, *Vertues Common-Wealth; or, The High-Way to Honour* (1603), signature Q2ᵛ.

[3] Dekker, Prologue, *If It Be Not Good the Devil Is in It* (1610–12), in Shepherd, ed., *Dramatic Works.*

be so martyred. And if he find her inclining to foolish pittie, as commonlie such women are, then he applies the matter to him-selfe, and saies that he is likewise caried awaie with the liking of her; crauing that pittie to be extended upon him, as she seemed to showe toward the afflicted amorous stager. . . . Credite me, there can be found no stronger engine to batter the honestie as wel of wedded wiues, as the chastitie of vnmarried maides and widowes, than are the hearing of common plaies.[4]

The writer is of the class apt to see dangers where few ex-isted, but his charge must not be repudiated entirely. Testi-mony almost identical with his has been offered in recent times concerning the effect of motion pictures. Elizabethan love scenes, compared with those to which we have become accustomed, seem unprovocative, but the young lovers in the old audiences had not been conditioned by modern stimulants: think of the artless lines that in still earlier days had spelled damnation for Paolo and Francesca! In 1709 the ladies seem to have been less responsive: note the curious extract from a letter by Sir John Perceval, who had just seen *Othello* in London:

It was there I had an opportunity of seeing what gave me as much concern as the very play itself, I mean a flat insensibility in every lady, as if tenderness were no longer a virtue in your sex. . . . I can remember when the ladies were better natured; now, like Dutchwomen, they can talk of indifferent things at a time when the tenderest passions of their whole frame are called upon.[5]

It is pleasant to think that the "wedded wiues" and "vn-married maides and widowes" in Shakespeare's original

---

[4] *Second and Third Blast of Retrait from Plaies and Theaters* (1580), in Hazlitt, ed., *English Drama and Stage*, pp. 142–43.
[5] Historical Manuscripts Commission, *Egmont MSS*, II, 240.

audience, even to the jeopardy of their honor, were more tender and did not talk of indifferent things when Desdemona murmured "Commend me to my kind lord."

A widespread ability to quote the plays indicates the attentiveness of the spectators. For instance there is the enthusiast

> that ne'er of ought did speak
> But when of plays or players he did treat.
> Hath made a commonplace book out of plays,
> And speaks in print, at least whate'er he says
> Is warranted by Curtain plaudities,
> If e'er you heard him courting Lesbia's eyes;
> Say (courteous Sir), speaks he not movingly
> From out some new pathetic Tragedy?
> He writes, he rails, he jests, he courts, what not
> And all from out his huge long scraped stock
> Of well penn'd plays.[6]

Although the custom of taking "table-books" [7] into the play-houses to assist the memory was not unknown, the ability to quote extended beyond the literate and cultivated spectators. Dekker speaks of plays that "euery punck and her squire . . . can rand out by heart they are so stale," [8] and Beaumont's Apprentice seems to have acquired quite a distinguished repertory.

An attentive audience with a large capacity for enjoyment and a high emotional susceptibility might seem all that players and playmakers could ask for. But we wish to

[6] Marston, *Scourge of Villanie* (1599), ed. Harrison, Bodley Head Quartos, III, No. XIII, 107.
[7] Beaumont and Fletcher, Prologue, *The Custom of the Country* (1619–22), in Glover and Waller, eds., *Works*.
[8] *Iests to Make You Merrie* (1607), in Grosart, ed., *Non-Dramatic Works*, II, 303.

know more. Granted that Shakespeare's audience loved plays and even "sweete words, equally ballanced," did it prefer great drama and fine poetry? Granted that it was responsive, did it respond best to what was most authentic? What were its powers of discrimination? What was its quality?

Contemporary comments upon the quality of the audience are abundant but extremely difficult to interpret. They provide us actually with a series of contradictions. The danger is that the critic or historian will make a selection of the consistent statements and build a case upon them, failing to realize that the statements he has rejected are equally consistent with each other and completely nullify his case. In the present section of my study I shall counterpoise the various contemporary comments. Since they tend to neutralize each other, the discussion in general is bound to seem confusing and negative in effect. But at the very end we shall leave opinion and return to fact, finding, I believe, a bit of firm ground at last.

The quality of spectators is usually referred to in Elizabethan times as their "understanding." The understanding of the spectators is frequently attacked, but we are never certain what portion of them is intended and what criteria the spokesman is bringing to bear. The penny patrons are the most frequent objects of attack, but the entire audience is lumped as the ignorant multitude and blasted with the identical terms applied to "groundlings" if it suits the writer's purpose at the moment. Thus Gosson, in his more severe mood, classified all playgoers as "the worste sort of people" who, because of their ignorance, their fickleness, and their fury, are "not to bee admitted in place of iudgement." [9] Puttenham is offended at the "naturall ignoraunce" of the people who love plays, but apparently because they are indifferent to such technical fine points of prosody as concern himself: they "haue at all times their eares so attentiue to the matter, and their eyes vpon the shewes of the stage that they take little heede of the cunning of the rime." [10] Webster, after *The White Devil* failed, brought his charge against a specific theatre and its clientele: the Red Bull was too open, too dark (and too empty), and "most of the people that come to that Playhouse, resemble those ignorant asses." [11] But the poets who consoled Fletcher for the failure of *The Faithful Shepherdess* were equally emphatic that the audience was "common," "rude," a "monster," and a "rout of niffles," [12] although the theatre in this case was a private playhouse. Dekker at some time must have been maltreated by the pit; he lashes out at plebeians with a fury unexplainable on the grounds of their mere incapacity —at "the Stinkards speaking all things, yet no man vnderstanding any thing." [13] He cannot withhold insults even from the printed versions of civic entertainments, which must be written simply, else the heads of the multitude "would miserably runne a wooll-gathering." [14]

The charge that the groundlings lacked understanding was made only when they had disliked the spokesman's

[9] *Playes Confuted in Fiue Actions* (1582), in Hazlitt, ed., *English Drama and Stage*, p. 183.

[10] *Arte of English Poesie* (1589), ed. Arber, English Reprints, No. XV.

[11] Address to the Reader.

[12] Commendatory verses by Beaumont, Field, Aston, and Jonson.

[13] *Strange Horse-Race* (1613), in Grosart, ed., *Non-Dramatic Works*, III, 340.

[14] *Magnificent Entertainment* (1604).

play or had liked that of his rival. It will be considered further in a moment. It must be viewed in relation to a similar charge, made as frequently and under the same circumstances, against the genteel section of the audience. Jonson is as loud as any against the "rude, and beastly claps"[15] of the multitude, but he is equally loud against

> base detractors, and illiterate apes,
> That fill vp roomes in faire and formall shapes.[16]

He inveighs against "fastidious impertinents,"[17] the "better, and braver sort of your people! Plush and Velvet-outsides! that stick your house round like so many eminences —Of clothes, not understandings?"[18] The rank and file do not always come off worst at the hands of the satirists. The formula for a good play dictated by Beaumont's Grocer is at least preferable to that dictated by Day's Gentleman. The Grocer wants to see Englishmen of low degree perform romantic prodigies, while the Gentleman demands bawdry and venery "an ell deepe and a fathome broad":

2 [GENT.].　　Well, Ile sit out the play . . . but see it be
　　baudy, or by this light I and all my friends will hisse.
PROL.　　You should not deale gentlemen-like with us els.[19]

---

[15] Dedication, *Volpone* (1605–6), in Herford and Simpson, eds., *Ben Jonson*.

[16] Prologue, *Poetaster* (1601), in *ibid.*

[17] Dedication, *New Inn* (1629), in *ibid.*

[18] Induction, *Magnetick Lady* (1632), in *ibid.*

[19] Day, Induction, *Isle of Gulls* (1606), in Bullen, ed., *Works.* Another of the gentlemen prefers lampoons upon citizens, while a third seems to have really noble tastes. That the upper classes were those chiefly delighting in "wantonness" in plays was asserted as early as 1580 in a courageous and interesting passage in *A Second and Third Blast of Retrait from Plaies and Theaters*, in Hazlitt, ed., *English Drama and Stage*, pp. 146–47.

The company of Gentlemen is just as peremptory as the Grocer's family, just as narrow in its demands and somewhat less amiable.

Sometimes the audience is condemned without distinction of class. Beaumont assures Fletcher that spectators in general are swayed only by externals:

> One company knowing they judgement lack,
> Ground their belief on the next man in black.
> Others, on him that makes signs, and is mute,
> Some like as he does in the fairest sute,
> He as his mistress doth, and she by chance.
> Nor wants there those, who as the Boy doth dance
> Between the Acts, will censure the whole Play;
> Some if the Wax-lights be not new that day;
> But multitudes there are whose judgment goes
> Headlong according to the Actors' cloathes.[20]

Middleton includes "mirth" and "passion" among the things delighting an audience, but he too stresses superficialities:

> How is't possible to suffice
> So many ears, so many eyes?
> Some in wit, some in shows
> Take delight, and some in clothes:
> Some for mirth they chiefly come,
> Some for passion,—for both some;
> Some for lascivious meetings, that's their arrant;
> Some to detract, and ignorance their warrant.
> How is't possible to please
> Opinion toss'd in such wild seas?
> Yet I doubt not, if attention
> Seize you above, and apprehension

---

[20] Commendatory verses to *The Faithful Shepherdess.*

You below, to take things quickly,
We shall both make you sad and tickle ye.[21]

The concluding lines provide the formula into which attacks upon the audience ultimately crystallized: the genteel spectators were uncoöperative, the plebeian spectators unintelligent. The formula is applied in explicit terms by Ben Jonson: "The people generally are very acceptiue and apt to applaud any meritable worke, but there are two sorts of persons that most commonly are infectious to a whole auditory." These are, first, "the rude barbarous crue, a people that haue no braines, yet grounded iudgements, these will hisse any thing that mounts aboue their grounded capacities"; and, second, "a few Caprichious gallants . . . they haue taken such a habit of dislike in all things, that they will approue nothing." [22] The condemnation is less all-inclusive of the elevated than of the "grounded" spectators at the moment, but in another mood Jonson finds more hope in those that "canst but spell" than in a "hundred fastidious impertinents." [23] Here, then, is the difficulty. The two classes of unsatisfactory spectators can be expanded at the will of the displeased playwright, or his modern interpreter, until the entire audience is embraced, and we are left puzzled about the identity of the "people generally" who were "very acceptiue and apt to applaud any meritable worke."

We are likely to go seeking, as the incentive to good writing, not the average but the exceptional member of the au-

---

[21] Prologue, *No Wit, No Help like a Woman's* (c.1613), in Bullen, ed., *Works.*

[22] *The Case Is Altered* (before 1609), Act II, Scene vii, in Herford and Simpson, eds., *Ben Jonson.*

[23] Dedication, *New Inn* (1629), in *ibid.*

dience—the "judicious" spectator. This alluring person is mentioned by Shakespeare's amateur of the drama: he "must in your allowance o'erweigh a whole theatre of others." [24] We hear of him again from Jonson:

> if I proue the pleasure but of one,
> So he iudicious be; He shall b' alone
> A Theatre vnto me: [25]

For the one or, at most, the few attentive and understanding auditors, Jonson purports to write:

> For these, Ile prodigally spend my selfe,
> And speake away my spirit into ayre;
> For these, Ile melt my braine into inuention,
> Coine new conceits, and hang my richest words,
> As polisht jewels in their bounteous eares.[26]

But on Jonson's pinnacle of Parnassus there is not always a foothold even for this select company, and the playwright must seek his crown only in "his owne free merit." [27]

That the creative artist in Shakespeare's age, as in all ages, sought the approbation of the best judges and of himself goes without saying. The difficulty lies in identifying these judges and in defining the forces which guided the artist in the formulation of his high personal standards. Our confidence in the "judicious" spectator is shaken when we discover that he is distinctly a party man: he qualifies for his place of lonely eminence just so long as he approves of the particular playwright's work; otherwise he becomes only

[24] *Hamlet* (c.1601), Act III, Scene ii, l. 25, ed. Furness, *New Variorum Edition*.

[25] To the Reader, *Poetaster* (1601), in Herford and Simpson, eds., *Ben Jonson*.

[26] Induction, *Every Man out of His Humor* (1599), in *ibid*.

[27] To the Reader, *Poetaster* (1601), in *ibid*.

"the Over-curious Critick." [28] Although practically no dramatic criticism found its way into print, there seems to have been no absence of critical attitudes. Plays were discussed in taverns and elsewhere, particularly in the theatres themselves. Gainsford speaks ironically of the nonpaying spectator: "He shall laugh as hartily, obserue as iudiciously, and repeat as exactly for nothing" as if he had paid, "Yea, you shall finde him able (or forward) in short time to correct the Actors, or censure the Poet." [29] Of the critical discussion provoked by their offerings, the playwrights show a considerable, and increasing, awareness, and they do not seem especially pleased. When Beaumont observes that

> One company, knowing they judgement lack,
> Ground their belief on the next man in black;

he obviously considers the man in black an incompetent and a dangerous bellwether. Chapman is quite severe with those who

>   in aim
> At higher objects, scorn to compose plays,
> (Though we are sure they could, would they vouchsafe it!) [30]

Dekker and Middleton have no love for those auditors who think

>   that each Scoene should be a booke,
> Compos'd to all perfection; each one comes
> And brings a play in's head with him: up he summes,

---

[28] Dekker, Prologue, *Wonder of a Kingdom* (1623), in Shepherd, ed., *Dramatic Works.*

[29] *The Rich Cabinet Furnished with Varietie of Descriptions* (1616), in Hazlitt, ed., *English Drama and Stage,* p. xi.

[30] Prologue, *All Fools* (1599–1604), in Parrott, ed., *Plays and Poems.* See also his foreword to *The Middle Temple and Lincoln's Inn Mask* (1613).

> What he would of a Roaring Girl haue writ;
> If that he findes not here, he mewes at it.[31]

Now unless we are to consider the "judicious" simply as the playwright's own little putative claque, we must suppose them to have been the spectators who applied standards and assumed the role of critics. How, then, are we to reconcile the contemporary irritation with critics and love of the "judicious"? In general, the playwrights rail at faultfinders and praise "the other sort, that heare with loue, and iudge with fauour." [32] We must take our choice of which sort qualified as the "judicious."

Plays which were "caviare to the general," which were directed to princes and other better judges, are a further trial to our faith in the "judicious" spectator. Daniel's *Philotas* was written "for the better sort of men, seeing with what idle fictions, and grosse follies, the Stage at this day abused mens recreations." [33] Jonson's *Cynthia's Revels* was not for "eu'rie vulgar, and adult'rate braine." [34] *Catiline* was a "legitimate Poeme" in "Iig-giuen times," [35] intended for scholars, not for those who "commend the two first Actes, with the people, because they are the worst." [36] These are meritorious plays, but they are not the masterpieces of the age or even of their several authors. In reading *Catiline*,

---

[31] Dekker, Prologue, *Roaring Girl* (1604–10), in Shepherd, ed., *Dramatic Works*.

[32] Epilogue, *Wily Beguiled* (1596–1606), ed. Greg, Malone Society Reprints.

[33] The Apology, *Tragedy of Philotas* (1604), in Grosart, ed., *Complete Works*.

[34] Prologue, *Cynthia's Revels* (1600–1601), in Herford and Simpson, eds., *Ben Jonson*.

[35] Dedication, in *ibid*.

[36] To the Reader in Ordinarie, *Catiline, His Conspiracy* (1611), in *ibid*.

we find our tastes coinciding with those of "the people." Yet these are about the best of the plays written avowedly for superior spectators. Such plays usually convey us into depressing purlieus. Consider a later effort by Jonson himself:

> A Worke not smelling of the Lampe, to night,
>   But fitted for your Maiesties disport,
>   And writ to the Meridian of your Court,
> Wee bring; and hope it may produce delight:
> The rather, being offered, as a Rite,
>   To Schollers, that can iudge, and faire report
>   The sense they heare, aboue the vulgar sort
> Of Nut-crackers, that onely come for sight.

The play thus recommended in its Prologue was only *The Staple of News*. I need not mention the academic plays or that whole body of courtly writing which I have elsewhere dubbed cavalier drama [37] and which scarcely achieved mediocrity.

The tendency to attribute the failure of plays to the deficiency of the audience, particularly the groundlings, must ultimately have amused the dramatic fraternity. After Hamlet speaks of the play which "pleased not the million; 'twas caviare to the general," although he and other better judges found it "excellent," a speech is recited proving that noble piece to have been an outrageous example of bombast. We should be placed on our guard against taking Hamlet's dramatic pronouncements as literally Shakespeare's, yet Hamlet's later remark that groundlings "for the most part are capable of nothing but inexplicable dumb-shows and noise" has often been quoted by those who blame upon ground-

---

[37] *Cavalier Drama*, pp. 7–47.

lings everything distasteful in Elizabethan plays. It is true that Hamlet at this later moment is in a more serious mood, but even if no satirical note is being sounded here, we must remember that the speaker is the Prince of Denmark, generically disdainful of groundlings. Yet times were changing: "By the Lord, Horatio," says Hamlet, moved by the wit of that indubitable groundling, the First Gravedigger, "these three years I have taken note of it; the age is grown so picked that the toe of the peasant comes so near the heel of the courtier, he galls his kibe." [38] All things can be proved by quoting Hamlet. Nowhere has Shakespeare suggested *in propria persona* that he has any quarrel with groundlings. The ironic note is clear enough in Day's *Isle of Gulls*. Warned that if he uses "a high and eleuate stile" in his projected play, his "auditories low and humble vnderstandings should neuer crall ouer't," a conceited buffoon replies: "Tush, I could fashion the bodie of my discourse fit to the eares of my auditorie: for to cast Eloquence amongst a companie of Stinctards is all one as if a man should scatter Pearls amongst the hoggish animals ecliped Swine." [39]

Out of the welter of comment upon the audience emerges one amusing fact. The most successful writers were the least critical of the spectators' powers of discrimination, and the less successful writers were less critical when they had

[38] Act V, Scene i, l. 132, ed. Furness, *New Variorum Edition*. It is doubtful if Shakespeare would have depended upon the patrons in the yard to distinguish between the playwright's opinion and that of his protagonist. Hamlet's speech sounds like the insult direct, and, after the opening of the private theatres, the groundlings must have been more valuable than ever to the Globe. We may note that the quarto of 1603 reads not "groundlings" but "the ignoraut"—probably a wise acting variant.

[39] Act III, Scene i.

scored a hit. Dekker can say, despite his low opinion of the
mob:

> 'Tis not a gay sute, or Distorted Face,
> Can beate his Merit off, Which has won Grace
> In the full Theatre.[40]

Even Jonson relaxes. In *Epicoene*, he wrote a play for everyone.

> Truth sayes, of old, the art of making plaies
>   Was to content the people; & their praise
>   Was to the Poet money, wine, and bayes.
> But in this age, a sect of writers are,
>   That, onely, for particular likings care,
>   And will taste nothing that is populare.
> With such we mingle neither braines, nor brests:
>   Our wishes, like to those (make publique feasts)
>   Are not to please the cookes tastes, but the guests.[41]

Jonson himself, earlier and later, professed membership in
that very "sect" he now condemns, but, like his original
audience, we are grateful for his periods of apostacy.

Honest Thomas Heywood was no railer at audiences.
The general tenor of his addresses is simply "We have
found you gracious Auditors." He is proud that his *Ages*
"haue at sundry times thronged three seuerall Theatres,
with numerous and mighty Auditories." [42] As with "our
prose Shakespeare," so with Shakespeare himself. He sub-
mits to judgment:

[40] Prologue, *Wonder of a Kingdom* (1623), in Shepherd, ed., *Dramatic Works.*
[41] Prologue, in Herford and Simpson, eds., *Ben Jonson.*
[42] To the Reader, *The Iron Age* (published 1632), in Pearson, ed.,
Dramatic Works.

Like, or find fault; do as your pleasures are:
Now good or bad, 'tis but the chance of war.[43]

His spectators are "gentles all" and are addressed pleasantly, unassumingly, respectfully. His tone is composed; the dramatist seems content. Invidious appraisals of the understanding of the auditors, or distinctions among them, are left to Hamlet or to the supercilious young collaborator John Fletcher.[44] In his sonnets Shakespeare lets fall a few words of discontent. He has "sold cheap what is most dear." Fortune has provided for him only "public means which public manners breeds," and his nature "like the dyer's hand" is stained by what it works in. Briefly, Shakespeare had moments of disgust with his own profession—as who has not? Similar sensations have overtaken professors in the refined atmosphere of their seminars, but unlike poets they do not tell all.

That Shakespeare could come to terms with his audience while Jonson could not reflects a basic distinction between the two men. Jonson was torn by his critical self-consciousness. His difficulty lay not in his independence of his audience but in his subjection to his idea of it. He refined upon his analysis of what it wanted and should have until his purposes became confused. He tried to write for sectors of the audience and found himself bobbing for green apples. The pronouncements of a critic like Jonson are tempting to later critics, but so far as they concern the audience they are full of mare's-nests. Not only can Jonson be quoted constantly against himself, but his words contain implications which might sometimes embarrass those who quote them. When

[43] Prologue, *Troilus and Cressida* (1601–3).
[44] Prologue, *Henry VIII* (1613).

he speaks of audiences commending "writers, as they do Fencers, or Wrastlers; who if they come in robustiously, and put for it with a great deal of violence, are receiu'd for the brauer fellowes," he has particular writers in mind; and when he distinguishes between those who "utter all they can, how euer unfitly; and those that use election and a meane," we begin to discern Jonson on one side of the line and Shakespeare—"would he had blotted a thousand"—on the other.

I deny not, but that these men, who alwaies seeke to doe more than inough, may some time happen on some thing that is good, and great; but very seldome: And when it comes it doth not recompence the rest of their ill. It sticks out perhaps, and is more eminent, because all is sordide, and vile about it: as lights are more discern'd in a thick darknesse, then a faint shadow. I speake not this, out of a hope to doe good on any man, against his will; for I know, if it were put to the question of theirs and mine, the worse would finde more suffrages: because the most favour common errors.[45]

Read in comparison with the famous passage on Shakespeare in *Timber or Discoveries,* the above leaves little doubt of whom Jonson had chiefly in mind. The measure of Jonson's generosity in finally conceding the greatness of Shakespeare is the effort it must have cost him. He had relapses and was never fully reconciled to the unchastened success of his great rival, to the preference shown by audiences for "some mouldy tale like Pericles." [46] In comforting Fletcher for the failure of *The Faithful Shepherdess,* Jonson had predicted that

---

[45] To the Reader, *Alchemist* (1610), in Herford and Simpson, eds., *Ben Jonson.*
[46] Ode to Himself, *New Inn* (1629), in *ibid.*

fire
Or moths shall eat what all these fools admire.

An appended list of the plays destined for oblivion would
have contained a fair number of titles by Shakespeare. A
list prepared by "all these fools" in the audiences would
have been more generous—and more prophetic.

It is not to the prologues, dedications, and epistles that
we must look for a fair evaluation of the quality of Shakespeare's audience. The complaining authors air too many
grievances, and their composite indictment, naming as it
does both the high and the low, the critical and the uncritical, is too all-inclusive. The only persons worthy of the
plays appear to have been the dedicatees, a small but superbly
discriminating sect. We must look about for those who,
perversely, appeared to appreciate good things.

We catch curious glimpses of a phenomenon that seems
to have bewildered the cultivated—of the mob responding
favorably to things too fine for their coarse intellects. The
gifted playwright

> Can draw with Adamantine Pen (euen creatures
> Forg'de out of th' Hammer, on tiptoe, to Reach vp,
> And (from Rare silence) clap their Brawny hands,
> T' Applaud, what their charmd soule scarce vnderstands.[47]

Appreciation from a quarter where appreciation presumably
could not be partook of the nature of the marvelous. The
term "charmed" is repeated in *The Actors Remonstrance or
Complaint*, where we hear of former playwrights "charm-
ing like Orpheus the dull and brutish multitude, scarce a
degree above stones and forrests, into admiration though

[47] Dekker, Prologue, *If It Be Not Good the Devil Is in It* (1610–12),
in Shepherd, ed., *Dramatic Works*.

not into understanding." [48] At Shakespeare's plays, so the printer tells us, even "dull and heauy-witted worldlings . . . haue found that witte there, that they neuer found in them selues, and haue parted better wittied then they came: feeling an edge of witte set vpon them, more then euer they dreamd they had braine to grinde it on." [49] This ability to rise to the plays seemed at least to one generous observer a thing natural and benign: Thomas Heywood considered it one of their virtues that they had made "the ignorant more apprehensive." [50]

Some slight opportunity for statistical analysis of the tastes of the audience is offered by Henslowe's *Diary* in the record of the yield of various plays during successive performances. Although the recorded yield is only that of the galleries, I believe that it fairly represents the preferences of the audience as a whole; but, unfortunately, few of the play runs are traced in their entirety and few of the play texts have survived for modern appraisal.[51] Nevertheless, if one compares the patronage of individual plays as suggested by gallery receipts, the results are revealing. In the chart which I append,[52] two periods of acting and fifteen extant plays are represented. We are uncertain of the relative age of the old plays, but, so far as we can judge, the most patronized plays are not necessarily the most recently written. The two most popular plays of the first period of acting, *The*

[48] In Hazlitt, ed., *English Drama and Stage*, p. 264.
[49] "A neuer writer, to an euer reader. Newes," *Troilus and Cressida* (1609, 2d issue).
[50] *Apology for Actors* (1612), Shakespeare Society Publications, No. III, pp. 52–53.
[51] Some of these few, *The Battle of Alcazar* for instance, may survive only in inferior texts. The merits of Marlowe's *Faustus* are apparent in spite of an inferior text.
[52] See Chart IV, Appendix B, p. 178.

Spanish Tragedy and *The Jew of Malta,* are still being performed in the second period. *The Battle of Alcazar,* probably, and *Henry VI,* Part I, certainly, have passed to theatres other than the Rose. *The Spanish Tragedy* seems to have been rated somewhat above its merits, and *Friar Bacon and Friar Bungay* somewhat below its merits, but in general the London playgoers were right about the plays. The number of their shillings supplies about the same "preferential rating" that our volumes of criticism have since supplied. Marlowe was preferred to his contemporaries, and Marlowe's better plays to his poorer. It has already been argued that Shakespeare was preferred to his contemporaries,[53] and the most fascinating of the plays now were the most fascinating then. That the chart is conclusive cannot be maintained, but like all the other evidence it throws the burden of proof upon anyone who believes that the Elizabethan playgoers rewarded mediocrity and penalized merit. Quite apart from any statistical demonstration, we know that the most gifted playwrights were recognized in their own generation, and by the many rather than by the few. The high quality of the plays was not purely gratuitous, and the writers in general might well have addressed the audience in the terms of Henry Porter: "Well Gentlemen, I cannot tell how to get your fauours better then by desert." [54]

[53] See pp. 47–51.
[54] Prologue, *Two Angry Women of Abington* (1598), ed. Greg, Malone Society Reprints.

VI

QUALITY: MODERN
APPRAISALS

WE HAVE NEARLY EXHAUSTED the supply of direct evidence on the nature of Shakespeare's audience.
There remain the diverse elements to be found in the plays
themselves. But here we confront a difficulty. Any approach to the audience through the plays must be highly
subjective; conclusions are as apt to reflect the nature of
the reader as of what he reads. That Shakespeare's plays
mirror the audience for which they were written, except in
their defects, has as often as not been dismissed as an im-
practical notion. The reason is understandable. The defects
are irritating, but it would be ungrateful merely to say so,
with the audience available as whipping boy. Of course, the
subjective element is bound to obtrude no matter what type
of evidence is being interpreted, including the figures in
Henslowe's *Diary*. The best we can do is to collect it and
leave the issue to debate.

What follows is my contribution to the debate. It is
mainly rebuttal, but its intention is constructive. Sarcastic

allusions to "commentators" come without grace from those who themselves are commenting. Shakespeare like Falstaff is the cause that wit is in other men, and the most brilliant criticism in English has been provoked by Shakespeare's plays. But the least brilliant of this criticism is, I believe, that which relates the plays to their audience. It is usually incidental; and it is often careless, cynical, or marked by an incredible condescension. The Elizabethan stratum of humanity is divested of mystery, its common sense assessed at the rate of some early treatise on physiology, its perceptive range simplified to "two levels of intelligence," while whole battalions of our former fellow mortals are dismissed with placid allusions to "groundlings" or "a motley crew." At the safe remove of three centuries the nature of a generation collectively has even been deduced from a heap of nutshells. Sometimes distance lends courage also to the idealist, and the Globe is filled with mute inglorious Shakespeares, but normally we hear the voice of derision and disdain. Not all of the critical attitudes toward the audience are uncongenial, but none of them need be taken on faith.

We are familiar with the tendency in others (and ourselves) to apply colors recklessly to any part of a canvas depicting the lusty age of Elizabeth. Enthusiastic brushwork transforms human beings into Elizabethans. A brief description of Shakespeare's audience by Brander Matthews contains the following phrases: "superabundant energy," "soaring imagination," "puffed with pride," "reckless daredevil," "sensuous and sensual," "furious in hate and love," "avid of swift sensation," "primitive savagery of manners," "violently passionate," "frankly brutal." [1] The portrait is ex-

---

[1] In *Shakspere as a Playwright*, pp. 294–312.

hilarating but conducive at last to sober reflection. Were Shakespeare's contemporaries truly such galvanic creatures? Imagine, if you will, some London carter plodding beside his oxen on the road to Hackney, some London housewife sewing a fine seam, some London mason patiently, skillfully pointing the stones of Bridge Gate at 1s. 4d. a long, long day. Imagine entering some Bread Street shop in 1601, fixing the proprietor with your eye, and saying: "You are puffed with pride, a reckless daredevil, furious in hate and love, violently passionate, and frankly brutal." Would he not reply with pardonable dismay: "Who? Me!" Nothing we can discover from examining their daily routine, their frugal expense accounts, and their quiet and sensible letters suggests that Elizabethans, individually or collectively, were vastly different from us. Their nature cannot be deduced from the defeat of the Armada or the public hangings in Tyburn. We ourselves live in a spectacular age, without being individually spectacular.

The kinship we feel with the old playgoers, those of us who love their drama, must not be confined to the upper classes, no matter what our own social allegiances or aspirations may be. I have previously quoted the statement that while Heywood wrote for apprentices and shopkeepers, Shakespeare "kept in his mind's eye the approval of the lordly patrons of Blackfriars." The writer, I suspect, would indignantly repudiate the implications of the statement if put in bald terms—the fine things in Elizabethan drama were written for the fine people, for lords. So prevalent is the notion that one is apt to countenance it through sheer inadvertence; the cloven hoof flashes out in half the Shakespearean criticism being written. Inadvertence can scarcely be the explanation for the following: "The movie seems to be quite as capable of proceeding on two levels as the Elizabethan tragedy: poetry and psychology for the gentlemen's galleries, action and blood for the pit." [2] The writer is a careful investigator in a modern field, repeating something evidently conceived to be a critical truism. But if we are to confuse social with spiritual distinction, we may as well subscribe at once to the belief that Shakespeare's plays were written by the Earl of Oxford, or Southampton, or Rutland, or whoever the current candidate may be.

Misconceptions are prevalent concerning the intellectual and artistic attainments of the Elizabethan nobleman. One suspects that he is often patterned in the image of Sir Philip Sidney and the Earl of Southampton, the latter generously endowed with the qualities found in the literary works dedicated to him. It is true that the English Renaissance brought forth lords, knights, and gentlemen with literary gifts, in greater number, perhaps, than any comparable span of years, but it was a great age and the law of averages was operating. It is doubtful if the proportion of the genteel classes displaying such gifts, creative or appreciative, was higher than that of the literate ungenteel. That the nobility could produce a Sidney is the less remarkable in view of the ability of the middle classes to produce a Spenser and a Milton. Marlowe and Shakespeare illustrate the remarkable efficaciousness of extraction from workers in leather. Many men of high birth still looked with disdain upon anything so clerkly as literature, while many others, including nominal patrons of now famous dramatic companies, displayed simply a depressing indifference. The Elizabethan great

[2] Thorp, *America at the Movies*, p. 23.

world from the queen down, let the truth be told, was mean to its poets and dramatists.

As we read Sir Edmund Chambers's fine volumes on the Elizabethan stage, we come first to the queen, then to the royal household, then to the Revels Office, until by this magnificent route we arrive at the theatres and the acting companies. All is relevant and all is revealing, but, unless we are wary, we may gather the impression that the drama of the age was an appendage of the court. An equally valid approach to the stage would be a chronicle of London taverns and of enterprisers before James Burbage. Sir Edmund writes:

It will be manifest, in the course of the present treatise, that the palace was the point of vantage from which the stage won its way, against the linked opposition of an alienated pulpit and an alienated municipality, to an ultimate entrenchment of economic independence.[3]

Let us not forget the spadesmen who dug that entrenchment, the anonymous thousands who dropped their pennies in the gatherer's box: these were the true patrons of Elizabethan drama. The queen, the Privy Council, and the (bribed) officials of the Revels Office sponsored a working arrangement whereby one minor means of her majesty's "solace" could be maintained at the public expense. It was quite unconsciously that the court performed its great service to art: poetry like Protestantism entered the palace through a postern gate.

Sir Edmund continues:

On the literary side, the milieu of the Court had its profound effect in helping to determine the character of the Elizabethan

---

[3] *Elizabethan Stage*, I, 3.

play as a psychological hybrid, in which the romance and erudition, dear to the bower and the library, interact at every turn with the robust popular elements of farce and melodrama.

But the specifications of the habitué of bower and library had to be modified by something other than farce and melodrama before great drama could result. The appearance of its qualities of greatness awaited that "ultimate entrenchment in economic independence" provided by the populace of London. The names of great lords had been associated with acting companies for generations before plays show signs of poetic or other artistic worth. The drama was as popular at court before the eighties as after, and, for all we know otherwise, *Herpetulus the Blue Knight and Perobia* was as cordially received there in 1574 as *King Lear* in 1606. No great Elizabethan play was written by a sojourner in the great world, and, so far as we know, such plays appealed no more to that world than to the public at large. In fact, the highborn as a class showed a preference for pageantry and pedantry, for pastoral and mask, and the body of drama they ultimately created for themselves was, above all else, fantastic. The bane upon Renaissance drama in Italy was its failure to escape from the palace and the library. Elizabeth and James permitted Shakespeare to write, but there was another kind of permission not within the royal gift—permission to write as he did.

In one sense Elizabethan drama was lordly indeed, or kingly: a throne was the one indispensable piece of theatrical property. Thoughts flew upward, and the multitude had to be treated to displays of majesty. Playwrights shared this taste for grandeur, and the fine people in their audience must have been stimulating. Noble auditors, like command

performances, would have given a cachet to dramatic activity. The lordly ones were still lordly; their functions
were not all deputized: they were lawgivers and leaders
in battle. They were personally imposing, so clad and attended as to give visible token of their power and affluence.
They were distinguishable and on view—we may owe them
something for that. Playwrights would have been conscious
of their presence, and ambition and vanity are great releasers
of energy.

It is even conceivable that some playwrights then, like
some critics now, assumed the minds of lordly patrons to
be as elegantly furnished as their bodies and for them, especially, hung out their "richest words as polisht jewels." But
it is hard to believe that we owe the poetry and psychology
of the drama to the accident of the writers' having been
dazzled. Shakespeare knew an Osric when he saw one, and
he knew that Osrics were more plentiful than Sidneys. *Hamlet* itself would not have been written for such courtiers as
it portrays. Assuming among the writers a willingness to
let the "candied tongue lick absurd pomp," would poetry
and psychology have resulted? or satire, "wantonness,"
pomposity itself? We do not know as we read what sad
jest may have been designed to tickle the Earl of Rutland,
or what lovely song to charm the groundlings. "Why should
the poor be flattered?" to ask Hamlet's question. Because
in Shakespeare's theatre there were so many of them.

This is not to imply that poetry and psychology were
wasted upon the "gentlemen's galleries." The patrician was
as capable of rising above his class as the plebeian. It is only
to insist, with weariness, that mentality should not be measured in terms of caste. If we substitute the word "taste"

for "mentality," we must reckon with what has been deduced as to the essential "unity of taste" among all castes, and among playwrights and playgoers together, in Elizabethan times.[4] To assume that action and bloodshed (or farce and wordplay) were intended exclusively for the pit is simply not feasible. The disparate elements in the drama —the bloodshed and sweeping action on the one hand and poetry and psychology on the other—are explainable on a sounder principle than that of dual appeal to social levels in the audience. The disparity may result from nothing more than a theatrical heightening of the actual contrast in life— between the constantly observable crudity of human action and refinement of human thought. Elizabethan drama is not the only great literature where the contrast is glaringly reflected. The soul stirrings of Achilles, kin of the gods, were necessarily infinite, but what he actually did was sulk in his tent or slay Trojans. The balance between the tendency to action and the tendency to reflection is more apt to be disturbed in favor of reflection among modern critical readers of Shakespeare than among Elizabethan playgoers (or human beings generally), so that the action of the plays is apt to seem intrusive. Naturally we wish to think of the nobility as sharing our tastes: we invite only the best people to join our club.

Sometimes Shakespeare's spectators are graded not according to a social hierarchy in his day but an intellectual hierarchy in ours. The "judicious" spectator is newly invoked, and he is endowed with the ability to discern in the play esoteric meanings not intended for the audience as a

[4] See Bradley, "Shakespeare's Theatre and Audience," *Oxford Lectures on Poetry;* and, especially, Sisson, *Le Goût public et le théâtre élisabéthain,* Chapter III (Unité du goût public).

whole; in default of either his or the playwright's having left a commentary, the modern critic supplies it. Spectacular results can be achieved by this method, and, strangely enough, the most spectacular of all has been achieved by one of the most meticulous of scholars. W. W. Greg distinguishes between the "bulk" or "generality" of Shakespeare's audience and the "humaner minds" and argues that the playwright wrote two meanings into *Hamlet:* the "humaner minds" perceived that Claudius was no murderer and the Ghost's accusations were "a mere figment of Hamlet's brain." Greg presents this theory with earnestness and skill; then later he defends it, although he has "never discovered" whether he believes in it himself.[5] These are baffling tactics. If one were to describe a newly found quarto of the play with a title page bearing an unknown printer's device, stipulating that what appeared to be the device might be after all only the stain of a crushed roach, Greg's indignation can be imagined.

Evidently it is only with the "unknowable," with the meaning of the book rather than with the book as a physical fact, that we may take liberties. Whether Greg believes in his theory is immaterial; he certainly believes in the two levels of intelligence and in the "judicious" spectator. Yet his theory has demonstrated once and for all the slippery nature of this person: we never know when we have him in hand. Originally, he was the occult friend of the playwright; he now serves the critic in a like capacity. So far as the meaning of *Hamlet* is concerned, Adams, Schücking,

---

[5] "Hamlet's Hallucination," *Modern Language Review*, XII (1917), 393–421; "Re-Enter Ghost: a Reply to Mr. J. Dover Wilson, *ibid.*, XIV (1919), 353–69; "What Happens in 'Hamlet,'" *ibid.*, XXXI (1936), 145–54.

Granville-Barker, W. W. Lawrence,[6] and presumably most others are content to stand with the "bulk" of the audience. But even if Greg had only a single opponent, J. Dover Wilson let us say, we should have to recognize that among the "humaner minds" in the audience, some were more human than others, and we should have to postulate not two levels of intelligence but three at least—Greg's, Wilson's, and the "generality's."

W. W. Lawrence has said that Shakespeare "provided for the more intellectual spectators something which the groundlings, with their imperfect mentality and defective education, could not perceive, but this was an extension of the simple meaning of his play, and not at variance with it." [7] With the main bearing of this statement, one must certainly agree. It is unfortunate, however, that perfection of mentality and adequacy of education seem still to be measured in ratio to distance from the ground. Are we not too facile in our generalizations about the education and mentality of the penny playgoers? It seems probable that the rank and file were more literate in the sixteenth century than in the eighteenth. In view of the profusion of schools,[8] of the tendency of the trade guilds to make literacy a qualification even for entrance into apprenticeship,[9] and of the manifest interest in self-instruction, we must revise any impressions we may ever have had that London workmen were

[6] For a review of the controversy and a restatement of his own sound position, see Lawrence, "Hamlet and the Mouse-Trap," *PMLA*, LIV (1939), 709–35.

[7] *Shakespeare's Problem Comedies*, p. 15.

[8] Knights, "Education and the Drama in the Age of Shakespeare," *Criterion*, XI (1931–32), 599–625. Most of the spectators at the Globe "were likely to have received an education of the Grammar school type" (p. 607), i.e., such as Shakespeare himself had received.

[9] Dunlop, *English Apprenticeship and Child Labour*, pp. 45, 136.

"nine-tenths illiterate." In a period of eight months during the single year 1585, the publishers disposed of ten thousand copies of their reading primer, *The A B C and Little Catechism*.[10] Using this book, women at their wheels and men at their looms taught, for a pittance, the children of other workers how to read. In the opinion of the one who has most carefully investigated the subject, the people of London constituted "by no means an illiterate society." [11] It would be impossible to prove that more than a fraction even of the groundlings in Shakespeare's audience had no passport to books.

The groundlings, nevertheless, like the audience in general, did not read much: books, candles, and daylight leisure were all hard to come by. The great majority of men and women were "ignorant." But we must ask whether ignorance was so crippling in the time of Shakespeare as it is today. There were, without doubt, more unlighted chambers in the mind of the average spectator than in our own, and creatures of darkness found a dwelling there, but we are likely to overestimate the degree of this benightedness. Miss Doran, in her excellent attempt to discover the Elizabethan attitude toward the ghost in *Hamlet*, has mentioned the "lack of relevance between fact and theory" [12] in Renaissance science. Cannot one say, without casuistry, that when theory is fallacious, the ignorant benefit by their enforced reliance upon observable fact? The burned child who shuns the fire has been an inductive philosopher for ages. It was

[10] Plant, *English Book Trade*, p. 40.
[11] Adamson, "The Extent of Literacy in England in the Fifteenth and Sixteenth Centuries: Notes and Conjectures," *Library*, Ser. IV, X (1929), 163–93.
[12] "On Elizabethan Credulity," *Journal of the History of Ideas*, I (1940), 166.

the learned ones who needed Bacon's recommendations. Edward Topsell was more "learned" about beasts than other Englishmen in 1607. But observe his earnest belief in the existence of the unicorn and his contempt for ignorant unbelievers:

the vulgar sort of infidell people which scarcely beleeue any hearbe but such as they see in their owne Gardens, or any beast but such as in their own flocks, or any knowledge but such as in their own braines, or any birds which are not hatched in their own Nests.[13]

We must score one for the "vulgar." Topsell was relying upon authority, the rank and file upon experience. We must not decide upon the attitudes and beliefs held by the rank and file of Elizabethans through reading their authorities. We must not assume that credulity, concerning unicorns, satyrs, or even ghosts and demons, was then the especial mark of the uncultivated as it is now.

J. Dover Wilson is quite assured in his pronouncements on what Shakespeare's audience believed about various things.[14] It would be folly to ignore the erudition and analysis of so talented a writer. Inquiry into contemporary point of view is the current fashion in Shakespearean criticism, and a wholesome one, but we must look twice at all the conclusions. The difficulty is that we cannot consult the spectators at the Globe and make sure they had read the right books. If a critic quotes selected passages from selected works to prove what the audience thought upon selected topics, we are likely to witness only a sinister alliance between the

[13] *The Historie of Foure-Footed Beastes* (1607), quoted in *ibid.*, p. 166.
[14] *What Happens in Hamlet, passim.*

pedantry of two ages. The following passage, I believe, does not aid in demonstrating that Hamlet was a man of action and would be so regarded by Shakespeare's audience:

Perhaps most significant is the statement by the illustrious French physician Laurentius, whose works were read throughout Western Europe: "The melancholike are accounted as most fit to undertake matters of weightie charge and high attempt. Aristotle in his Problemes sayeth that the melancholike are most wittie and ingenious. . . ." If then ability to transact important business was one result assigned to the melancholy temperament, this temperament could hardly have been looked upon as causing morbid inaction. Why then did Shakespeare make Hamlet melancholy? [15]

There is always the possibility that both Shakespeare and his audience had formed an opinion about melancholy otherwise than by reading Laurentius.

An amusing revelation of the practical responses of the audience is offered by the fate of *The Faithful Shepherdess.* Fletcher complained that the audience, noting that the characters were shepherds, but "missing whitsun ales, creame, wasiel & morris-dances, began to be angry." [16] In a word, they wanted the shepherds to behave like shepherds. To them it meant nothing that the play obeyed, in Chapman's words of praise, "the holy lawes of homely pastorall." Unlike Chapman, they were ignorant of such laws. We see the force in operation again in *The Knight of the Burning Pestle.* When Merrythought in the play says, "Never trust a Tailor that does not sing at his work; his mind is of nothing but

---

[15] Draper, *The Hamlet of Shakespeare's Audience,* pp. 177–78. I question the premise of the concluding statement in the book: "Shakespeare's audience was an audience of men, and Shakespeare's Hamlet was a man's Hamlet."
[16] To the Reader.

filching," the Grocer's wife in the audience comments, "Mark this George, 'tis worth noting: Godfrey my Tailor, you know never sings, and he had fourteen yards to make this gown; and I'll be sworn, Mistress Penistone the Draper's Wife had one made with twelve." [17] Here is dramatic criticism in its purest form.

The most invidious modern charge against Shakespeare's audience is that it was primitive, brutal, in some way spiritually debased. It is not infrequently made. In mild form the charge appears in the following passage forming part of an otherwise closely reasoned treatise on the acting time of Elizabethan plays:

> Would this audience, composed largely of illiterate Londoners, be able without excess of mental and physical fatigue, to concentrate its undivided attention for three hours without a break upon such an enthralling melodrama as *Richard III* or such a soul-stirring tragedy as *Othello?* Could such primitive beings pay out the nervous energy needed to endure three hours of imaginative exaltation? The very rapidity of the actors' utterance must have imposed a tiresome strain upon untrained minds, toiling in vain to keep pace with speeches not half understood. [18]

The atmosphere created is suggestive of the Old Stone Age; evolutionary processes seem to have been marvelously accelerated since Shakespeare's day. We may be dealing here only with indiscretion of speech. Such cannot be said of the following, included in the most recent study of Shakespeare's audience, and inspired by the putting out of Gloucester's eyes and by other "horrors" in the plays:

[17] Act II, Scene i.
[18] Hart, "The Time Allotted for Representation of Elizabethan and Jacobean Plays," *Review of English Studies*, VIII (1932), 412.

What these horrors enable us to do is accurately to measure the sensibility of the audience and to gauge their imaginative reaction. On that evidence we have no choice but to rate both low. This deduction is, of course, amply borne out by our knowledge of the time. A strong vein of brutality and an insensitiveness to physical suffering were part and parcel of the mentality of the Elizabethan audience.

Miss Byrne's summing up presents the "psychological picture" of "an audience primitive and undeveloped imaginatively." [19]

The most furious assault upon the audience on the grounds of spiritual and moral depravity was made by Robert Bridges:

Shakespeare should not be put into the hands of the young without the warning that the foolish things in his plays are for the foolish, the filthy for the filthy, and the brutal for the brutal; and that, if out of veneration for his genius we are led to admire or even tolerate such things, we may be thereby not conforming ourselves to him, but only degrading ourselves to the level of his audience, and learning contamination from those wretched beings who can never be forgiven their share in preventing the greatest poet and dramatist of the world from being the best artist. [20]

A. C. Bradley, the poet laureate's good and even deferential friend, could not let these words pass wholly unrebuked, although in the traditional manner of scholars, he placed the disagreeable matter in a footnote and almost in Latin. [21]

[19] Byrne, "Shakespeare's Audience," in Shakespeare Association, *A Series of Papers on Shakespeare and the Theatre*, pp. 200, 215.

[20] "On the Influence of the Audience," *The Works of William Shakespeare* (Shakespeare Head Press ed.), X, 334.

[21] *Oxford Lectures on Poetry*. He is "not always repelled" by the things condemned in Mr. Bridge's "very interesting and original con-

Bridges's essay as a whole scarcely invites refutation. The details considered "filthy," "foolish," and "brutal" are of a type to be found also in nondramatic works such as few members of the popular audiences could have afforded to buy. The words themselves are too harsh. To share Bridges's attitude toward the audience, we must share his view that Falstaff was at last bidden a "triumphant farewell" by a creator recoiling in moral disgust; we must be willing to exchange Falstaff as he is for Falstaff as Bridges would have him. There is an obvious risk in endorsing a conception of the audience based upon such details of the plays as "most offend the simple taste" of a particular critic, no matter how eminent he may be; fortunately, scolding the audience is an alternative to excising the plays.

That our "knowledge of the time," as Miss Byrne maintains, establishes the presumption of "a strong vein of brutality and an insensitiveness to physical suffering" is a courageous assertion, placing a tremendous burden upon our knowledge of the time. Miss Byrne is identifying Elizabethans with certain of their institutions. We must consent, presumably, to be identified with certain of ours. The children once harnessed to coal carts in the tunnels of English mines should send us seeking brutality in the poetry of Coleridge and Wordsworth. If we do not find it, perhaps we should wonder how these poets could have been so brutally aloof. It is easy to cast stones. Children are harnessed no more, but evils still are permitted to exist. It would be an indiscretion of taste to mention some of these

---

tribution" and suggests "reasons for at least diminishing the proportion of defect attributable to a conscious sacrifice of art to the tastes of the audience" (p. 367, note 4).

[152]

evils, since we have become so sensitive, so ingenious in evading the spectacle of suffering, so convinced of the ethical superiority of looking the other way.

Each age has its own brutalities. The Elizabethans were forced to live more intimately with theirs, and they acceded to the conditions of their existence. Shakespeare's auditors look at Talbot spattered with stage blood; but as they look, they weep. Throngs gather to see the felons hanged at Tyburn, but "the criminals' friends come and draw them down by their feet, that they may die all the sooner." [22] Is this brutality or tenderness? Animals are baited and whipped in the pits, but voices are raised in protest and the sport is declining.[23] Beneath its "callouses" human nature must have been the same in Shakespeare's day as in ours. The range of feeling must have been the same. People are still compounded of heaven and earth: kind fathers are harsh creditors, decent folk exchange ribaldries, and ruffians rescue puppies. We need to know more about human impulses in all ages before we grow rash about the Elizabethans. We need to distinguish between what is fundamental in human nature and what is superficial adjustment to environment. Perhaps the whole range of impulses was more operative in the less comfortable age of Shakespeare and more apt to impress itself upon art. It is more accurate to say that the audience expected and accepted brutality than that they de-

[22] *Thomas Platter's Travels in England, 1599,* p. 174.

[23] Bearbaiting and bullbaiting were cruel, but they were enjoyed not as cruelty but as sport. There were a conflict of forces and a sharing of risks. The activity was more lethal to the dogs than to the bulls, and even the men who whipped the bears took serious risks. Baiting was sometimes for "her Majesty's disport," and interest in it was not a matter of class distinction. Not the "brutal" element but the "sporting" element was attracted. The attitude toward animals, shared by Shakespeare himself, was still strictly utilitarian.

manded and enjoyed it. There is a manifest injustice in charging Shakespeare's audience with brutality because of the putting out of Gloucester's eyes, unless we credit it with an exquisite tenderness because of Lear's words over the body of Cordelia.

Among the hosts of books about Shakespeare's plays, some are ignorant and foolish; one can always make a Roman holiday by quoting such books. I have avoided doing so, at the cost of comic relief. The only alternative has involved a certain injustice; one never represents fairly the views of responsible writers by quoting a few vulnerable statements. I have not pretended to evaluate in their entirety the essays I have quoted, but to illustrate from them some of the commoner attitudes toward Shakespeare's audience. That these attitudes may be mistaken is illustrated by opposing counsel. The treatment by Thorndike, although deficient in proof and perhaps mistaken in details, strikes me as essentially true.[24] Bradley, although almost in wonder, affirmed that "The audience had not only imagination and the power to sink its soul in the essence of drama. It had something else of scarcely less import for Shakespeare, the love of poetry." [25] Elmer E. Stoll, in his most recent utterance, rejects the judicious few:

by ear the audience through lifelong attendance responded to the niceties of the different art in the Forum and the Athenian and London theatres. The technique as such they did not understand; but the ideas, sentiments, and morals, the language and situations, were not above their heads, and to what they heard they were accustomed, attuned.[26]

[24] *Shakespeare's Theater*, pp. 404–31.
[25] *Oxford Lectures on Poetry*, p. 392.
[26] "Poetry and the Passions: an Aftermath," *PMLA*, LV (1940), 982–83.

Felix E. Schelling holds no brief for lordly patrons:

The drama of Shakespeare and his immediate fellows spoke to men by right of their manhood, not by virtue of their gentility. It stirred in its appeal the depths of a large and generous humanity.[27]

And Charles J. Sisson points out that most of those qualities with which Beaumont mockingly endowed his citizen-grocer —patriotism, personal pride, love of romance, and the rest —can, in the "spectateur représentatif," scarcely be considered undesirable.[28]

The "representative spectator" may be as much an abstraction as the "typical man," but conveniences must sometimes be used. We may say in the present case, quite apart from Beaumont's satirical use of them as the spectators in *The Knight of the Burning Pestle*, that a grocer, his wife, and their young apprentice form as acceptable an epitome of Shakespeare's audience as any the facts will warrant us to choose. If Shakespeare did not write to please such a little cockney family as this, he did not write to please his audience. But if he did so write, then there must be some correspondence in quality between the plays and our sample three—the grocer, his wife, and their young apprentice.

Reflection may reduce our amazement. That the potentialities of the human mind are unaffected by time, place, and social position is sound biology, and we may safely presume that our little group possessed human minds. We may even presume that they possessed the right kind of minds. We find them in the theatre separated from many of their neighbors —the stolid, the material, the bigoted, the folk of predomi-

[27] *Elizabethan Drama*, I, xxxviii.
[28] *Le Goût public et le théâtre élisabéthain*, pp. 52–65.

nately animal appetite. That they had read few books is no stigma upon them. The modern correspondence between the reading habit and active mentality is a product of new folkways. Even complete illiteracy, when not the product of incapacity or indifference, but of mere conformity, may be consonant with the highest intelligence, sometimes even with heightened powers of memory and observation.

The minds of our spectators have been sharpened by urban life. The cockney as a type has seldom been accused of stupidity. In 1601 London is growing rapidly, teeming with life and variegated activity. As like as not our little group are first generation Londoners, as stimulated and knowledgeable as modern New Yorkers lately transplanted from their prairie homes. In any case, in the crowded London of 1601 alertness is a condition of survival.

They are easy in the company of the audible arts. Music, preaching, speechmaking, storytelling, disputation—these have been available even when food and warmth have not. There is lacking the tremendous range of diversions and distractions to be devised by later centuries, but there is always the spectacle of humanity, the balm of melody, the marvel of words. The theatres have been standing a lifetime, offering an education in literature and history. Wide vistas have been opened to the mind and have furnished it with powers of association. The unlearned have been taught "the knowledge of many famous histories" and few playgoers are "of that weake capacity that cannot discourse of any notable thing." [29]

The factor above all else that we must reckon with in

[29] Heywood, *Apology for Actors* (1612), Shakespeare Society Publications, No. III, pp. 52–53.

assessing the quality of our sample spectators is the almost incalculable effect of interest upon understanding. We have all been amazed at the proficiency of small boys in analyzing batting averages and of certain of their elders, dense in every other way, in moving easily through technical labyrinths concerning their business. Let us assume that our three spectators are intensely interested in plays. Of course, our instincts may still instruct us that no one out of a London shop could possibly have appreciated *Hamlet*—just as no one out of a Stratford shop could possibly have written it.

VII

OUR SHAKESPEARES AND
OUR AUDIENCES

I DID NOT ENGAGE to solve the mystery of Shakespeare's audience, and I have not done so. But to dwell thus long with a subject without dogmatizing a little at last would be to display an inhuman restraint: I add the following generalities as a personal indulgence.

I believe that Shakespeare's audience was a large and receptive assemblage of men and women of all ages and of all classes. If I were set down in old London and startled by the novelty of the event, I should make for the Globe and huddle there in confident security until I could recover my aplomb. Surrounding me would be cheerful and decent folk who had come singly, in mixed couples, in family parties, wearing their Sunday best. The place would be so quiet, despite the throng standing on the ground and packed along the benches in superimposed grandstands, that the chief intrusion upon my nervous reflections would be the voices of the actors on the stage. What the people about me might be thinking and feeling, it would be impossible to discover.

Their remarks would not tell me much. My own remarks in a theatre, always and even to me, sound flat and unprofitable.

I should guess that the audience as a whole understood and appreciated what it bought and approved. Its approval could not have been easy to win. Unlike some other audiences existing in and near his time, Shakespeare's audience was literally popular, ascending through each gradation from potboy to prince. It was the one to which he had been conditioned early and for which he never ceased to write. It thrived for a time, it passed quickly, and its like has never existed since. It must be given much of the credit for the greatness of Shakespeare's plays. Mere coincidence will not explain why every Elizabethan play addressed to a sector of the people, high or low, learned or unlearned, is inferior in quality; why neither university, nor law school, nor guild hall, nor princely banquet house begat dramatic poetry comparable to what came from the public theatres; or why Blackfriars failed to sustain the level achieved at the Globe. The drama reached its peak when the audience formed a great amalgam, and it began its decline when the amalgam was split in two. The difference between Shakespeare and Fletcher is, in some inverse fashion, the difference between a penny and sixpence.

To grant the audience our respect is reasonable enough. The genius of Shakespeare was incredibly great, but so also is the genius of men by and large. When Bradley said that he would prefer a glimpse into Shakespeare's mind to a chance to mingle with the spectators at the Globe,[1] he was poising the contents of one book against the cover of an-

---

[1] *Oxford Lectures on Poetry*, pp. 361–62.

other. A fairer alternative choice would be a glimpse into the collective mind of the audience. Perhaps that is what a glimpse into Shakespeare's would be. His plays were not wholly dissociated from other phenomena. The tendency to consider them so has encouraged the tendency to view their author as a ghost. Although few of us any longer are inclined to regard Shakespeare as merely the most brilliant star in a bright constellation, we should not discard the residuum of truth in such a conception. His drama was no different in kind from that of his fellows, and its quality realized an ideal elsewhere perceptible. The quality of the drama rose in gradations through the work of lesser men and the lesser work of Shakespeare himself to reach its peak in individual scenes in individual masterpieces. These were part of the whole, the crest of the ground swell. The height of the crest of quality measures the strength of the propulsive forces acting from below. These forces had their place of origin. They must have generated among Shakespeare's fellowmen, and they must have operated through his audience. How can we ignore this obvious reciprocity? If Shakespeare exerted the greatest power over the audience, it follows that the audience exerted the greatest power over him. It follows that he expressed it best.

There is no need to magnify the individual spectator. All that Shakespeare had to offer was immediately apparent to him no more than it is to us. He was willing to accept on the average much less than Shakespeare offered. But he preferred Shakespeare. This is the fact that we must cling to. He found in these plays room for his soul at its widest dimension. He preferred too much to too little. He could grasp some things, touch others, and sense the presence of

[160]

more. Each intelligence is of individual size and shape. Each spectator comprehends the main intent of the play and more or less of its subtleties, according to his capacity. The subtleties missed by one are not missed by his neighbor. The reception of the play is a work of collaboration. Shakespeare's meanings are caught in the mesh of a thousand minds.

George G. Coulton, whose humane spirit has survived his long sojourn in an era when the families of plain people were referred to as "broods" and "litters," has said that "there is more latent poetry in a stock broker or a soapboiler than all that is expressed in Shakespeare's plays." He is discussing the popular ballads, a "People's Literature . . . limited but never falling below a certain standard." [2] The broadside ballads of the sixteenth and seventeenth centuries, that is, the ballads written for the people, fall far below the standard of those which, in a sense, had been written by the people. The broadside ballads are no gauge of the artistic preferences of the people. They were made to sell at a price. Had the gifted lyrists of Elizabethan times offered their compositions at two sheets for a penny, they would have found a lively market. The balladmongers would not have been driven from the field, but the average quality of the poetry purchased would have maintained that "certain standard" apparent in the "People's Literature." The theatrical audience pooled its pennies, and the Elizabethan play as compared with the Elizabethan broadside illustrates the advantages of collective bargaining. Shakespeare's plays were a people's literature in a truer sense than were even the authentic popular ballads; and they were, therefore,

[2] *Medieval Panorama*, p. 102.

less limited. The "people," as it signifies only the masses, is itself an exclusive term. A lord or a scholar, like a carter, is one of the people, and a Senecan tragedy, like a folktale, is part of the people's lore.

A study of Shakespeare's audience should reveal those conditions most likely to render operative the latent poetry in men. We must notice that it was large enough to sample Shakespeare's generation, but although it was large it was selective. The principle of selection was susceptibility to the appeal of dramatic and poetic art. Playgoing was not mandatory or even especially convenient, and thousands stayed away. We must recognize that poetry is so latent in some people as to amount only to a theoretical probability. But most important of all, Shakespeare's audience was socially, economically, educationally heterogeneous. It was motley, and for this we must be thankful.[3] An audience so mixed compelled the most discerning of all authors to address himself to men and not to their badges, to men's intelligence and not to its levels. The influence upon the individual exerted by class, whether high or low, is a cramping influence, narrowing the horizon, warping the sympathies, prejudicing the mind. But where all classes are there is no class; there is that common humanity which subtends all. To the kind of audience for which he wrote, and to the fact that he did write for it, we owe Shakespeare's universality. We are amused at the ease with which his work escapes the sectarian and partisan. It now resists Marxian exegesis as readily as in the past it has resisted appropriation by the

[3] We should wish it had been even more so. Perhaps if the preachers had mingled in the audience instead of railing outside, another and beneficial stress would have been exerted upon the playwrights.

elite. It belongs to everyone because it was created for everyone. It was created for man—"how noble in reason! how
infinite in faculty! . . . how like an angel in apprehension!
how like a god!" No individual or class can claim to have
sat for this portrait. It represents man in the large, and
Shakespeare's huge and heterogeneous audience was man in
the large.

If it be objected that great art may be created for other
than a universal audience or reading public, that Shakespeare himself despatched "sugred sonnets among his pri-
uate friends," that *Paradise Lost* was in no sense a best seller,
we need only define our terms. The art of the few is great,
when great it is, not because of but in spite of its exclusiveness. The qualities of artistic greatness in the literature of
the few are identical with those in the literature of the many.
The simplest products of the fundamental forms of literary
expression—singing, storytelling, play-acting—can encompass as much art as a Vergilian epic. They encompass less
intellectuality. Milton's learning became part of the very
texture of *Paradise Lost,* but the poem is great not because
of its learning but because of Milton's triumphant reduc-
tion of it in his crucible; he scaled Olympus with his fardel
on his back. The poem is inaccessible to the uncultivated
reader because of its learning, not because of its art. Such
works must take their chance with posterity, whatever contemporary critics may prophesy for them. Critics have been
notoriously deficient as prophets of immortality. Normally,
the work which has the best chance of survival is the one
which appeals, if not to the most people, at least to the most
kinds of people in its own age. If it pleases all in one age, it
will please some in all ages.

Our attitude toward those for whom Shakespeare's plays were written must affect our attitude toward the plays themselves and must increase or decrease our pride of possession. Dazzled by Shakespeare's eminence and our individual awareness of it, we are apt to grow disdainful of all outside our small communion and to belittle the "generality." But if the audience at the Globe were the "generality," then so are we—we are simply belated arrivals. If we withdraw the opprobrious terms and concede the audience a share in the merit of the plays, we add to our own stature and our right to glory in our kind. It is an opportunity not lightly to be dismissed. None of us can show a warrant over Shakespeare's hand to leave our place in the audience and to join him in his study.

Sir Edmund Chambers, in a recently published "Epilogue" to his years of fruitful research into Shakespeare's life and stage, disheartens me with what seems to be a disgust with the whole world of the theatre. He is "dreaming a little," he says, and by a process perhaps "alien to the strict canons of scholarship," he makes the poet retire early from the tainted atmosphere of London and its playhouses to dwell amidst the flowers of Stratford. "Here, among the young mulberries he had planted, he could write his plays, send them, as Parson Ward tells us, to the stage at the rate of two a year, and never trouble about what happened to them afterwards." [4] The dream, however beautifully expressed, is one I should not wish to share. It bedecks Shakespeare with funeral garlands before his time. We cannot deny that weariness and defeat may have overtaken the

[4] "William Shakespeare: an Epilogue," *Review of English Studies*, XVI (1940), 400–401.

poet in his middle years so that he distinguished invidiously between God's creatures, preferring flowers to men, but I should suppose him to have been more robust—and more grateful. London had rescued him from Stratford, and the theatres had made him more than he had had any reasonable hopes of becoming: his garden was a field of upturned faces. We must overcome our own repugnances rather than make Shakespeare share them.

Ultimately Shakespeare's audience will make us think of audiences now. Are our audiences getting what they deserve? Would plays be better if audiences were other than they are? It is, of course, hazardous for those of us who have been "dwelling in the past" to speak of the present. Perhaps we are enamored and place a fanciful value upon the power and poetry we seem to discern in Shakespeare; or perhaps such power and poetry, or their artistic equivalent, are actually appearing in contemporary plays but find us blind, just as some of Shakespeare's coevals were so absorbed in Plautus and Seneca that they missed what was happening at the Globe; or perhaps we are dwellers in a ghost town, and the mental and even aesthetic energies of our day course through new thoroughfares so that some future age will view a steel press not only as a triumph of the human intellect but as a thing of amazing beauty. One can admit the theoretical tenability of any of these suppositions without relinquishing an unassailable position. Whatever else we are creating, we are also creating drama—more abundantly than ever before in human history—and it is our natural desire that it should be worthy of our generation.

I have heard the poverty of modern drama roundly rebuked and prescriptions offered for its enrichment: new

Portias would appear on our stages if we could bring back the boy actors, new Othellos if we could resuscitate the stock company; new beauties would return to dramatic dialogue if we could banish the box set; we must become more primitive and less commercial. Actually, however, the Elizabethans were less primitive and more commercial than we imagine; and the mere externalities of theatrical usage have little to do with the essence of drama. Shakespeare triumphed over the physical limitations of his stage and capitalized them; we could do likewise with ours, including the plethora of scenery, other factors being equal. It is even illogical to complain that we lack a Shakespeare. The English-speaking peoples have grown fiftyfold since the sixteenth century, and the law of averages is in our favor. Someone with his potentialities must be wailing in a crib right now. But competitive examinations and fellowships in creative writing will not bring the new Shakespeare to heel unless the place is prepared for him.

Audiences today in the legitimate theatre are by no means a cross section of humanity. The spectators may be called, for want of a better name, intellectuals or literati. If an accidental collision at the Globe would have brought us fact to face with a grocer, an accidental collision in a theatre today would bring us face to face with a schoolteacher. This modern audience is by no means a bad one. The intellectual has a wide range of sympathies and much power of association. He has some knowledge of all classes and can identify himself with them imaginatively. But an audience of this kind is only a reflection of a universal audience and is likely to be regaled only with reflections of universal plays. The moving-picture clientele is truly universal. The Lord Cham-

berlain's Men barnstormed in the provinces and acted in
Whitehall. Moving pictures are shown in the backwoods
and in the presidential mansion. In theory, at least, it is to
Hollywood that we should look for new dramatic triumphs.
But, unluckily, the moving-picture clientele does not com-
pose an audience at all. It does not participate in the creation
of a play, and its influence upon creative artists is exercised
through deputies not of its own choosing. The true audience
of a moving picture is a delegation of studio critics. Their
difficulties are considerable, for the diverse elements con-
stituting that humanity whose tastes they try to gauge form
an amalgam in no one theatre but are distributed in com-
plex patterns. It is little wonder that Hollywood's aim is
confused. It is interesting to notice that Chaplin and Disney,
the Hollywood creators who have permitted the fewest
intermediaries to come between them and their public, are
the truest artists and the most generally approved.

A universal audience and an immediacy of relationship
between audience and artist may be conditions impossible
to recover. Even in Shakespeare's day these conditions were
a felicitous accident. One truth remains by which we may
be both warned and comforted: the human fabric has not
deteriorated, and it is as vain to inveigh against our generation as against Shakespeare's. Under the right conditions
the "people generally" are still "very acceptiue." Their
capacity to respond to what is great and beautiful remains
undiminished, if less frequently exercised. It was impossible
to produce anything too good for the race in Shakespeare's
day, and it is equally impossible now. It is an arrogant man
indeed who writes down to mankind, and he hits always
below the mark.

APPENDIXES

Appendix A

ESTIMATES OF ATTENDANCE

T. W. BALDWIN's estimates occur in "Posting Henslowe's Accounts," *Journal of English and Germanic Philology*, XXVI (1927), 73, and in *The Organization and Personnel of the Shakespearean Company* (1927), pp. 172–73. A ratio is derived in the article and utilized in the book, to the effect that the average receipts at the outer door of the Rose Theatre were about seven-tenths those in the galleries. Before he could derive this ratio, the author had to identify a mysterious column of figures in *Henslowe's Diary* (ed. W. W. Greg [1904–8], I, 51–54) as representing the receipts at the outer door, entered daily by Henslowe alongside of his customary entries of the half-receipts of the galleries. This previously unidentified column of figures runs from January 24 to November 5, 1597, and by simply reducing each daily item to pennies, Baldwin purports to inform us of the total attendance at each performance within the period specified, since the fee at the outer door was a single penny. Comparison of the number of penny admissions with the gallery admissions also enables Baldwin, as he believes, to inform us which plays were popular with the "lower classes" and which with the "upper classes."

I believe, however, that we may state categorically that the column of figures in question does not represent the receipts at the outer door. The fluctuations in the daily sums bear no relation whatever to those in the daily sums collected in the galleries, and the divergences are so great as to create absurdities if Baldwin's theory were to be accepted. Thus, on March 23, 1597, at the performance of *Nabucadnazer*, 3*d*. are entered in the column, meaning presumably that 3 people only entered the theatre through the outer door. But from that fraction (of these 3 people) who elected to pay an additional 1*d*. and enter the galleries, 10*s*. were collected. Again, on March 12, when the old play *Valteger* was performed, £9 1*s*. 4*d*. appears in the column under scrutiny, meaning that 2,176 persons entered through the outer door. But only 36*s*. were collected in the galleries, meaning that no more than 432 of the 2,176 persons could possibly have proceeded from the yard to the galleries. That leaves 1,744 persons standing in the yard, and the Rose must literally have bulged! We need not inquire why 2,176 persons entered the Rose on one day and only 3 on the other, eleven days later. Less spectacular but equally damaging evidence that the second column of figures has nothing to do with the take at the outer door are the sums entered beside opening performances. Throughout the *Diary* gallery receipts go up inevitably on opening days, but the sums entered on such days in the column of figures supposed by Baldwin to represent receipts at the outer door are, in every instance but one, smaller than the average in the column as a whole. As to what the second column of figures in the *Diary* actually does represent, I, like the editor, do not know.

The late Ashley H. Thorndike's estimate occurs in *Shakespeare's Theater* (1916), p. 407: "There were often five or six theatres giving daily performances, which would mean that out of a city of one hundred thousand inhabitants, there were thirty thousand or more spectators at the play within a week." The estimate seems not to be very seriously intended, but it has serious implications, for if 30,000 out of 100,000 inhabitants of a city went to a theatre weekly, every inhabitant would be an habitual theatregoer. Actually, the statement is based upon a *non sequitur*.

As the number of theatres increase, the number of spectators in each need not remain constant. Moreover, there were rarely five or six theatres giving daily performances in Shakespeare's time. The author's figure for the population of London, 100,-000, also requires comment: earlier (p. 37) he had given 200,-000, illustrating the danger of thinking of London as the City at times and as the City and its suburbs at others. Certainly the figure that should have been used in connection with the 30,000 was the author's 200,000.

W. W. Greg's estimate of the size of the audiences at the Rose is very tentatively offered and does not claim or possess any validity (see p. 24). An estimate by Alwin Thaler is appended to *From Shakspere to Sheridan* (1922). The average capacity of Elizabethan playhouses is reduced to about 1,500 and the size of audiences to match. The figures are presented in a spirit of compromise, and I find them attractive, or did so at the outset of my study; however, any consistent piecing together of the actual evidence, such as it is, suggests that both theatres and audiences were larger than Thaler believes.

Appendix B

ATTENDANCE CHARTS

I. WORKDAYS [1]

Many daies of honest trauel are turned into vaine exercises
. . . poor men liuing by their handie labor are by them
trained vnto vnthriftines; scholars by their gaudes
are allured from their studies.[2]

Ordinary Day (28.18) ▬▬▬▬▬▬▬▬
Opening Day (54.49) ▬▬▬▬▬▬▬▬▬▬▬▬▬▬▬▬

Monday (31.38) ▬▬▬▬▬▬▬▬▬
Tuesday (29.17) ▬▬▬▬▬▬▬▬
Wednesday (25.41) ▬▬▬▬▬▬▬
Thursday (27.41) ▬▬▬▬▬▬▬▬
Friday (27.69) ▬▬▬▬▬▬▬▬
Saturday (21.30) ▬▬▬▬▬▬

Last Weekday
of Month (19.94) ▬▬▬▬▬▬

[1] The averages of Henslowe's receipts are given in shillings to two decimals. Ordinary days and opening days are averaged for the entire period covered by the accounts. The days of the week and last days of the month are averaged from June, 1594, through July, 1596, with opening days and holidays skipped.

[2] From *A Second and Third Blast of Retrait from Plaies and Theaters* (1580), in Hazlitt, ed., *English Drama and Stage.*

II. HOLIDAYS [1]

And trust me I am of that opinion, that the Lord is neuer
so il serued as on the holie-daies. For then hel
breakes loase. Then wee permit our
youth to haue their swinge.[2]

Average Day (30.16)

New Year's Day (52.60)
Epiphany (53.75)
Shrove Tuesday (41.00)
Ash Wednesday (44.33)
Easter Monday (42.25)
Easter Tuesday (48.75)
Easter Wednesday (47.00)
May Day (43.33)
Whitmonday (59.50)
Whit-Tuesday (59.00)
Whitwednesday (49.75)
Allhallows Day (46.33)
First Weekday after Christmas (56.75)
Second Weekday after Christmas (61.25)
Third Weekday after Christmas (50.00)

[1] The averages of Henslowe's receipts are given in shillings to two decimals. The average day is computed from every performance recorded in
the accounts. For the holidays, each average derives from at least three
occurrences (usually four or five) of the holiday in question.
[2] From *A Second and Third Blast of Retrait from Plaies and Theaters*
(1580), in Hazlitt, ed., *English Drama and Stage.*

III. THE SEASONS [1]

They are alwaies eating, & neuer satisfied: euer seeing, &
neuer contented; continualie hearing, & neuer wearied;
they are greedie of wickednes, and wil let no time,
nor spare for anie weather (so great is their
deuotion to make their pilgrimage) to
offer their penie to the Diuel.[2]

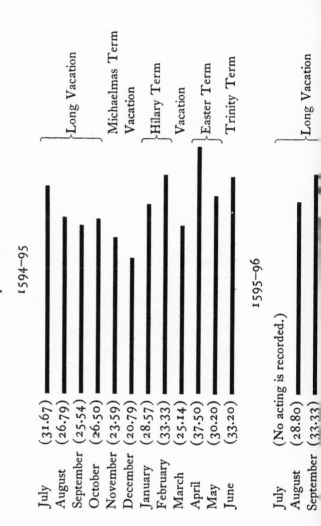

1594–95

July	(31.67)
August	(26.79)
September	(25.54)
October	(26.50)
November	(23.59)
December	(20.79)
January	(28.57)
February	(33.33)
March	(25.14)
April	(37.50)
May	(30.20)
June	(33.20)

Long Vacation

Michaelmas Term

Vacation

Hilary Term

Vacation

Easter Term

Trinity Term

1595–96

July	(No acting is recorded.)
August	(28.80)
September	(33.33)

Long Vacation

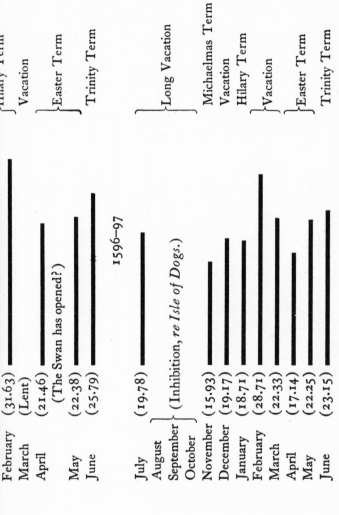

February (31.63)
March (Lent)
April (21.46)

(The Swan has opened?)

May (22.38)
June (25.79)

1596–97

July (19.78)
August
September } (Inhibition, *re Isle of Dogs.*)
October

November (15.93)
December (19.17)
January (18.71)
February (28.71)
March (22.33)
April (17.14)
May (22.25)
June (23.15)

Hilary Term
Vacation
Easter Term
Trinity Term

Long Vacation

Michaelmas Term
Vacation
Hilary Term
Vacation
Easter Term
Trinity Term

[1] The averages of Henslowe's receipts are given in shillings to two decimals. Opening days and holidays have been omitted since the number of these vary within each month and would obscure the trend if averaged in. Legal terms and vacations began and ended within months and usually according to the dates of movable feasts, but their span has been roughly indicated.

[2] From *A Second and Third Blast of Retrait from Plaies and Theaters* (1580), in Hazlitt, ed., *English Drama and Stage.*

IV. AUDIENCE APPROVAL [1]

At Stage Plaies . . . the worst sort of people haue the hearing of it, which in respect of there ignorance, of there
ficklenes, of there furie, are not to bee admitted in place of iudgement.[2]

Strange's Men—February 19, 1592, to February 1, 1593

Old
- Spanish Tragedy (602)
- Jew of Malta (568)
- Battle of Alcazar (481)
- Friar Bacon and Friar Bungay (126.75)
- Looking Glass for London and England (115)

New
- Henry VI, Part I (344.9)
- Knack to Know a Knave (265)

} First Seven Performances

Admiral's Men—June 15 [17], 1594, to July 28, 1597

Old
- Doctor Faustus (584)
- Tamburlaine, Part I (480)
- Jew of Malta (475.6)
- Spanish Tragedy (282)
- Tamburlaine, Part II (270)
- Massacre at Paris (258.5)

New
- Humorous Day's Mirth (562)
- John a Kent? "Wise Man of West Chester" (515)
- Blind Beggar of Alexandria (479)
- Captain Thomas Stukeley (279)

} First Ten Performances

---

[1] Henslowe's receipts are shown in shillings for all performances of old plays within each period and for as many performances of new plays as may be equated. Chapman's *Humorous Day's Mirth* was even more popular than the chart indicates, because its excellent run began in a period when receipts in general were falling off. The varying number of the performances of the old plays and the fact that some fell on holidays have been disregarded, since we are here interested in gross receipts—in how much the traffic would bear.

[2] From Gosson, *Playes Confuted in Fiue Actions* (1582), in Hazlitt, ed., *English Drama and Stage.*

LIST OF WORKS CITED

LIST OF WORKS CITED

For their courtesy in permitting me to quote from copyrighted works, I wish to thank the Clarendon Press, Malone Society, American Philosophical Society, Modern Language Association of America, Shakespeare Head Press, Jonathan Cape, Chicago University Press, Duke University Press, Houghton Mifflin Company, and the editors of the *Review of English Studies*.

Actors Remonstrance or Complaint, The: for the Silencing of Their Profession and Banishment from Their Severall Play-Houses (1643), in William C. Hazlitt, ed., The English Drama and Stage under the Tudor and Stuart Princes, 1543–1664. London, 1869.

Adams, Joseph Q. Shakespearean Playhouses: a History of English Theatres from the Beginnings to the Restoration. Boston, 1917.

Adamson, J. W. "The Extent of Literacy in England in the Fifteenth and Sixteenth Centuries: Notes and Conjectures," *Library*, Ser. IV, X (1929), 163–93.

Baldwin, Thomas W. The Organization and Personnel of the Shakespearean Company. Princeton, 1927.

—— "Posting Henslowe's Accounts," *Journal of English and Germanic Philology*, XXVI (1927), 42–90.

Baskervill, Charles R. The Elizabethan Jig and Related Song Drama. Chicago, 1929.

Beaumont, Francis, and John Fletcher. The Knight of the

[181]

Burning Pestle (c. 1607), The Faithful Shepherdess (1608), The Custom of the Country (1619–22), in Arnold Glover and A. R. Waller, eds., The Works of Francis Beaumont and John Fletcher. 10 vols. Cambridge, 1905–12.

Bentley, Gerald E. "The Diary of a Caroline Theatergoer," *Modern Philology*, XXXV (1937–38), 61–72.

Beveridge, Sir William. Prices and Wages in England from the Twelfth to the Nineteenth Century. London, 1939.

Bradley, Andrew C. Oxford Lectures on Poetry. London, 1909.

Brett-James, Norman G. The Growth of Stuart London. London, 1935.

Bridges, Robert. "On the Influence of the Audience," in The Works of William Shakespeare. 10 vols. Stratford-on-Avon, Shakespeare Head Press, 1904–7.

Byrne, Muriel St. Clare. "Shakespeare's Audience," in Shakespeare Association, A Series of Papers on Shakespeare and the Theatre. London, 1927.

Calendar of the Inner Temple Records, A, ed. F. A. Inderwick. 3 vols. London, 1896–1901.

Chamberlain, John. The Letters of John Chamberlain, ed. Norman E. McClure. 2 vols. Philadelphia, 1939.

Chambers, Sir Edmund K. The Elizabethan Stage. 4 vols. Oxford, 1923.

—— "Elizabethan Stage Gleanings," *Review of English Studies*, I (1925), 182–86.

—— "William Shakespeare: an Epilogue," *Review of English Studies*, XVI (1940), 385–401.

—— William Shakespeare: a Study of Facts and Problems. 2 vols. Oxford, 1930.

Chapman, George. All Fools (1599–1604), in Thomas M. Parrott, ed., The Plays and Poems of George Chapman. 2 vols. New York, 1910–14.

Chettle, Henry. Kind-Harts Dreame (1592), in Clement M. Ingleby, ed., Shakspere Allusion-Books, New Shakspere Society Publications, Ser. IV, No. I, Part I. London, 1874.

LIST OF WORKS CITED

Cheyney, Edward P. A History of England, from the Defeat of the Armada to the Death of Elizabeth. 2 vols. New York, 1914–26.

Clode, Charles M., ed. Memorials of the Guild of Merchant Taylors. London, 1875.

Collier, John P. The History of English Dramatic Poetry to the Time of Shakespeare. 3 vols. London, 1831.

Corbin, John. "Shakespeare and the Plastic Stage," *Atlantic Monthly*, XCVII (1906), 369–83.

Coulton, George G. Medieval Panorama: the English Scene from Conquest to Reformation. New York, 1938.

Creighton, C. "The Population of Old London," *Blackwood's Magazine*, CXLIX (1891), 477–96.

Crosse, Henry. Vertues Common-Wealth; or, The High-Way to Honour. London, 1603.

Daniel, Samuel. The Tragedy of Philotas (1604), in Alexander B. Grosart, ed., The Complete Works in Verse and Prose of Samuel Daniel. 5 vols. London, 1885–96.

Davenant, Sir William. The Unfortunate Lovers (1638), in James Maidment and W. H. Logan, eds., The Dramatic Works of Sir William D'Avenant. 5 vols. Edinburgh, 1872–74.

Davies, Sir John. The Complete Poems of Sir John Davies, ed. Alexander B. Grosart. 2 vols. London, 1876.

Day, John. The Isle of Gulls (1606), in Arthur H. Bullen, ed., The Works of John Day. London, 1881.

Dekker, Thomas. The Roaring Girl (1604–10), The Whore of Babylon (c. 1606), If It Be Not Good the Devil Is in It (1610–12), The Wonder of a Kingdom (1623), in Richard H. Shepherd, ed., The Dramatic Works of Thomas Dekker. 4 vols. London, 1873.

—— The Seuen Deadly Sinnes of London (1606), Newes from Hell (1606), Iests to Make You Merrie (1607), The Dead Tearme (1608), The Guls Horne-Booke (1609), The Rauens Almanacke (1609), Worke for Armourours (1609), Lanthorne and Candle-Light (1609), A Strange

Horse-Race (1613), in Alexander B. Grosart, ed., The Non-Dramatic Works of Thomas Dekker. 5 vols. London, 1884–86.

"Diaries and Despatches of the Venetian Embassy at the Court of King James I, in the Years 1617, 1618," *Quarterly Review*, CII (1857), 398–438. Translated by Rawdon Brown.

"Diary of the Journey of Philip Julius, Duke of Stettin-Pomerania, through England in the Year 1602," eds. Gottfried von Bülow and Wilfred Powell, in *Royal Historical Society Transactions*, New Series, VI (1892), 1–67.

Doran, Madeleine. "On Elizabethan Credulity," *Journal of the History of Ideas*, I (1940), 151–176.

"Dramatic Records from the Lansdowne Manuscripts," eds. Sir Edmund K. Chambers and W. W. Greg, in *Malone Society Collections*, I, Part II (1908), 143–215.

"Dramatic Records of the City of London: the Remembrancia," eds. Sir Edmund K. Chambers and W. W. Greg, in *Malone Society Collections*, I, Part I (1907), 43–100.

"Dramatic Records of the City of London: the Repertories, Journals, and Letter Books," ed. Sir Edmund K. Chambers, in *Malone Society Collections*, II, Part III (1931), 285–320.

Draper, John W. The Hamlet of Shakespeare's Audience. Durham, 1938.

Dunlop, Olive J. English Apprenticeship and Child Labour: a History. New York, 1912.

First Part of Jeronimo, The (1604–5), in Robert Dodsley, A Select Collection of Old English Plays, ed. William C. Hazlitt. 15 vols. 4th ed., London, 1874–76.

Fletcher, John. *See* Beaumont, Francis, and John Fletcher.

G.[ainsford?], T. The Rich Cabinet Furnished with Varietie of Descriptions (1616), in William C. Hazlitt, ed., The English Drama and Stage under the Tudor and Stuart Princes, 1543–1664. London, 1869.

Gawdy, Philip. Letters of Philip Gawdy of West Harling,

Norfolk, and of London to Various Members of His Family, 1579–1616, ed. Isaac H. Jeayes. London, 1906.

Gayton, Edmund. Festivous Notes on Don Quixote (1654), excerpts in John P. Collier, The History of English Dramatic Poetry to the Time of Shakespeare. 3 vols. London, 1831.

Gosson, Stephen. Playes Confuted in Fiue Actions (1582), in William C. Hazlitt, ed., The English Drama and Stage under the Tudor and Stuart Princes, 1543–1664. London, 1869.

—— The Schoole of Abuse (1579), ed. Edward Arber. English Reprints, No. III. London, 1868.

Graves, Thornton S. "Notes on Puritanism and the Stage," Studies in Philology, XVIII (1921), 141–69.

—— "Some References to Elizabethan Theaters," Studies in Philology, XIX (1922), 317–27.

Greene, Robert. The Second and Last Part of Connycatching (1591), The Thirde and Last Part of Connycatching (1592), in A. V. Judges, ed., The Elizabethan Underworld. London, 1930.

Greg, W. W. "Hamlet's Hallucination," Modern Language Review, XII (1917), 393–421.

—— "Re-Enter Ghost: a Reply to Mr. J. Dover Wilson," Modern Language Review, XIV (1919), 353–69.

—— "What Happens in Hamlet," Modern Language Review, XXXI (1936), 145–54.

Harbage, Alfred. Cavalier Drama: an Historical and Critical Supplement to the Study of the Elizabethan and Restoration Stage. New York, 1936.

Hart, Alfred. "The Time Allotted for Representation of Elizabethan and Jacobean Plays," Review of English Studies, VIII (1932), 395–413.

Harvey, Gabriel. Gabriel Harvey's Marginalia, ed. G. C. Moore Smith. Stratford-on-Avon, 1913.

Henslowe, Philip. Henslowe Papers, Being Documents Supplementary to [His] Diary, ed. W. W. Greg. London, 1907.

Henslowe, Philip. Henslowe's Diary, ed. W. W. Greg. 2 vols. London, 1904–8.

Heywood, Thomas. An Apology for Actors (1612), Shakespeare Society Publications, No. III. London, 1841.

—— The Iron Age (published 1632), in John Pearson, ed., The Dramatic Works of Thomas Heywood. 6 vols. London, 1874.

Historical Manuscripts Commission. The Manuscripts of the Earl of Egmont. 2 vols. London, 1905–9.

—— The Manuscripts of His Grace the Duke of Rutland. 4 vols. London, 1888–1905.

James I. The Political Works of James I, ed. Charles H. McIlwain. Cambridge, Mass., 1918.

Jones, P. E., and A. V. Judges. "London Population in the Late Seventeenth Century," *Economic History Review*, VI (1935–36), 45–63.

Jonson, Ben. Every Man in His Humor (1598), Every Man out of His Humor (1599), Cynthia's Revels (1600–1601), The Poetaster (1601), Volpone (1605–6), The Case Is Altered (before 1609), Epicoene (1609), The Alchemist (1610), Catiline, His Conspiracy (1611), The New Inn (1629), The Magnetick Lady (1632), in Charles H. Herford and Percy Simpson, eds., Ben Jonson. 6 vols. Oxford, 1925–38.

Judges, Arthur V., ed. The Elizabethan Underworld. London, 1930.

King, Gregory. "Natural and Political Observations and Conclusions upon the State and Condition of England," in George E. Barnett, ed., Two Tracts by Gregory King. Baltimore, 1936.

Knights, L. C. "Education and the Drama in the Age of Shakespeare," *Criterion*, XI (1931–32), 599–625.

Knoop, Douglas, and J. P. Jones. The Mediaeval Mason: an Economic History of English Stone Building in the Later Middle Ages, and Early Modern Times. Manchester, 1933.

Lane, John. Tom Tell-Troths Message, and His Pens Complaint (1600), ed. Frederick J. Furnivall, New Shakspere Society Publications, Ser. VI, No. II. London, 1876.

Lawrence, William J. The Elizabethan Playhouse and Other Studies. 2 vols. Stratford-on-Avon, 1912–13.

—— Those Nut-Cracking Elizabethans: Studies of the Early Theatre and Drama. London, 1935.

Lawrence, William W. "Hamlet and the Mouse-Trap," *PMLA*, LIV (1939), 709–35.

—— Shakespeare's Problem Comedies. New York, 1931.

Lyly, John. Campaspe (c. 1584), Sapho and Phao (c. 1584), Midas (c. 1589), in R. Warwick Bond, ed., The Complete Works of John Lyly. 3 vols. Oxford, 1902.

Lynd, Robert S., and Helen M. Lynd. Middletown. New York, 1929.

Marston, John. Antonio and Mellida (1599–1600), Antonio's Revenge (1599–1601), ed. W. W. Greg, Malone Society Reprints. Oxford, 1921.

—— Jack Drum's Entertainment (1600), in H. Harvey Wood, ed., The Plays of John Marston. 3 vols. Edinburgh, 1934–39.

—— The Scourge of Villanie (1599), ed. G. B. Harrison, Bodley Head Quartos, No. XIII, Vol. III. London, 1925.

Matthews, Brander. Shakspere as a Playwright. New York, 1913.

Meres, Francis. Palladis Tamia, Wits Treasury. London, 1598.

Middlesex County Records, ed. John C. Jeaffreson. 4 vols. London, 1886–92.

Middleton, Thomas. No Wit, No Help like a Woman's (c. 1613), in Arthur H. Bullen, ed., The Works of Thomas Middleton. 8 vols. London, 1885–86.

Nashe, Thomas. Pierce Penilesse, His Supplication to the Divell (1592), Christs Teares over Ierusalem (1593), in Ronald B. McKerrow, ed., The Works of Thomas Nashe. 5 vols. London, 1904–10.

Nef, John U. "Prices and Industrial Capitalism in France and England, 1540–1640," *Economic History Review*, VII (1936–37), 155–85.

Overbury, Sir Thomas. The Overburian Characters, Percy Reprints, No. XIII. Oxford, 1936.

Peacham, H. The Worth of a Penny (1647, for 1641), in Edward Arber, ed., An English Garner. 8 vols. London, 1877–97.

Perkins, William. "Cases of Conscience," in The Workes of that Famous and Worthy Minister of Christ in the Universitie of Cambridge, Mr. William Perkins. 3 vols. London, 1613.

Plant, Marjorie. The English Book Trade: an Economic History of the Making and Sale of Books. London, 1939.

Platter, Thomas. Thomas Platter's Travels in England, 1599. London, 1937. Translated by Clare Williams.

Porter, Henry. The Two Angry Women of Abington (1598), ed. W. W. Greg, Malone Society Reprints. Oxford, 1912.

Powell, Thomas. Tom of All Trades (1631), ed. Frederick J. Furnivall, New Shakspere Society Publications, Ser. VI, No. II. London, 1876.

Public Record Office. Calendar of State Papers, Venice and Northern Italy, 1615–1617. London, 1908.

Puttenham, George. The Arte of English Poesie (1589), ed. Edward Arber, English Reprints, No. XV. London, 1869.

Queenes Maiesties Proclamation for Staying of All Vnlawfull Assemblies in and about the Citie of London, The, July 4, 1595.

Return from Parnassus, The, Part II (1601–1603), in William D. Macray, ed., The Pilgrimage to Parnassus with the Two Parts of the Return to Parnassus. Oxford, 1886.

Rogers, James E. T. A History of Agriculture and Prices in England. 7 vols. Oxford, 1866–1902.

Rosenfeld, Sybil M. Strolling Players and Drama in the Provinces, 1660–1765. Cambridge, 1939.

Rowe, John. Tragi-Comoedia: Being a Brief Relation of the Strange, and Wonderfull Hand of God Discovered at Witny, in the Comedy Acted There February the Third, when there Were Some Slaine, Many Hurt, with Severall Other Remarkable Passages. Oxford, 1653.

Rye, William B. England as Seen by Foreigners in the Days of Elizabeth and James the First. London, 1865.

Schelling, Felix E. Elizabethan Drama, 1558–1642. 2 vols. Boston, 1908.

Second and Third Blast of Retrait from Plaies and Theaters, A (1580), in William C. Hazlitt, ed., The English Drama and Stage under the Tudor and Stuart Princes, 1543–1664. London, 1869.

Shakespeare, William. Hamlet (c. 1601), ed. Horace H. Furness, A New Variorum Edition of Shakespeare. 2 vols. Philadelphia, 1877.

—— The Works of William Shakespeare, ed. William A. Wright. 9 vols. London, 1891.

Sisson, Charles J. Le Goût public et le théâtre élisabéthain jusqu'à la mort de Shakespeare. Dijon, 1922.

Stage-Players Complaint, The, in a Pleasant Dialogue between Cane of the Fortune and Reed of the Friers (1641), in William C. Hazlitt, ed., The English Drama and Stage under the Tudor and Stuart Princes, 1543–1664. London, 1869.

Steele, Mary S. Plays and Masques at Court during the Reigns of Elizabeth, James and Charles. New Haven, 1926.

Stoll, Elmer E. "Poetry and the Passions: an Aftermath," PMLA, LV (1940), 979–92.

Stow, John. A Survey of London, ed. Charles L. Kingsford. 3 vols. Oxford, 1908–27.

Stubbes, Phillip. The Anatomie of Abuses (1583), ed. Frederick J. Furnivall, New Shakspere Society Publications, Ser. VI, No. VI. London, 1879.

Tawney, A. J., and R. H. Tawney. "An Occupational Cen-

sus of the Seventeenth Century," *Economic History Review,*
V (1934–35), 25–64.

Taylor, John.   The Trve Cavse of the Water-Mens Suit concerning Players, in Charles Hindley, ed., The Old Book
Collector's Miscellany.   3 vols.   London, 1871–73.

Thaler, Alwin.   From Shakspere to Sheridan: a Book about
the Theatre of Yesterday and To-Day.   Cambridge, Mass.,
1922.

Thorndike, Ashley H.   Shakespeare's Theater.   New York,
1916.

Thorp, Margaret F.   America at the Movies.   New Haven,
1939.

United States Bureau of Labor Statistics.   *Monthly Labor Review,* LI (1940), 474.

Ward, Sir Adolphus W.   A History of English Dramatic Literature to the Death of Queen Anne.   3 vols.   2d ed., New
York, 1899.

Webster, John.   The White Devil (c. 1612), in Frank L.
Lucas, The Complete Works of John Webster.   4 vols.
London, 1927.

Wheatley, Henry B.   London, Past and Present: Its History,
Associations, and Traditions.   3 vols.   London, 1891.

Wilson, Frank P.   The Plague in Shakespeare's London.
Oxford, 1927.

Wilson, J. Dover.   What Happens in Hamlet.   Cambridge,
1935.

Wily Beguiled (1596–1606), ed. W. W. Greg, *Malone Society Reprints.*   Oxford, 1912.

Wright, James.   Historia Histrionica (1699), in Robert Dodsley, A Select Collection of Old English Plays, ed. William
C. Hazlitt.   15 vols.   4th ed., London, 1874–76.

Wright, Louis B.   Middle-Class Culture in Elizabethan England.   Chapel Hill, 1935.

Wyburne, Joseph.   The New Age of Old Names.   London,
1609.

INDEX

INDEX

INDEX

Audience, Shakespeare's (*Cont.*)
powers of discrimination, 121
ff.; preferences expressed in
yields of plays, 135; responsiveness of unintellectual portion,
134; riotousness, 101-8; selective nature, 42-44, 162; self
control in disasters, 105; size,
19-52; social heterogeneity, 83-
86, 162; three types, 90; women
in, 74-79; youthfulness of, 79-
83, 90

Audience, universal, creation of
art for, 163; impossible under
modern conditions, 167; responsible for universality of Shakespeare's plays, 162

Audience approval, of plays at
Rose Theatre, 178

Authors, income, 61

Baldwin, T. W., 20, 171

Ballads, broadside, 59, 161; popular, 161

Baskervill, Charles R., quoted, 10

Battle of Alcazar, The (Peele),
136, 178

Bear baiting, 17, 57, 78, 84, 96

Bear Garden, 21, 57; collapse of,
78, 84, 106

Beaumont, Francis, commendatory
verses to *The Faithful Shepherdess*, quoted, 124, 127; *The
Knight of the Burning Pestle*,
characters in, 43, 53, 79, 82,
108, 120, 123, 149, 150, 155

Behavior, of audience, 92-116

Benedictines, 72

Berkeley, Lord, 107

Blackfriars Theatre, 37, 87, 88,
89; accused as focus of disturbance, 15; quality of drama
at, 159

Blind Beggar of Alexandria
(Chapman), 178

Boxes, 25

Boy companies, 36, 37, 108

Bradley, A. C., 151, 154, 159

Bridges, Robert, quoted, 151

Broadsides, 59, 161

Brothels, 57, 68, 91

Brutality, alleged characteristic of
Shakespeare's audience, 150-54

Burbage, James, 141

Burbage, Richard, 35, 110

Busino, Father, 86, 113; quoted,
78, 100

Byrne, Muriel St. Clare, 152;
quoted, 151

Capacity of theatres, 20-23, 29-34

Captain Thomas Stukeley, 178

Careless Shepherdess, The (Goffe),
quoted, 64-65

Caroline audiences, 110

Catholics, attitude toward theatre, 70

Catiline (Jonson), 128

Chamberlain, John, 70, 76, 80;
quoted, 85

Chambers, Sir Edmund, 6, 104,
164; *Elizabethan Stage*, quoted,
5, 75, 93, 141, 142

Chaplin, Charles, 167

Chapman, George, 149; *All-Fools*,
quoted, 127; *Blind Beggar of
Alexandria*, 178; *Humorous
Day's Mirth*, 7, 178

Chettle, Henry, 8; *Kind-Harts
Dreame*, quoted, 16-17, 102

Children, in audience, 79

Children's companies, 36, 37, 108

Cirencester, 54

Coarseness in drama, 10

Cockney, 156

Comedy, appreciation of, 117

[194]

INDEX

INDEX

INDEX

Pallant, Arthur, quoted, 73

Pallant, Robert, quoted, 73

Pamphleteers, 112

Paris Garden, *see* Bear Garden

Parliament, restrains profanity on stage, 8

Paul's Theatre, 88, 89

"People's Literature," 161

Pepys, Samuel, 43

Perceval, Sir John, quoted, 118

Pericles (Shakespeare), 87

Perkins, Richard, quoted, 73

Perkins, William, 69

Philip Julius, Duke of Stettin-Pomerania, 87; "Diary . . . ," quoted, 77-78

Philipo and Hippolito, 51

Pickpockets, 92, 96

Platter, Thomas, 26, 35, 76, 86; *Thomas Platter's Travels in England*, quoted, 24, 77

Playbooks, cost, 11

Players, accused of catering to plebeians, 13; good feeling between public and, 110

Playgoers, number, 41-44

Plays, appraisal by yield, 135; cost and earnings, 52; failure attributed to deficiences of audience, 129; new, attendance at, 28, 42, 46; written for superior spectators, 128; *see also* Drama, Elizabethan; *and under author*

Playwrights, awareness of criticism by audience, 127; opinion of audience, 122-34

Poetaster (Jonson), quoted, 126

Population of London, 38-41; analysis by classes, 54; within walking distance of theatres, 53

Porter, Henry, 136

Preachers, protest competition of theatres, 17

Prices, admission, scale of, 24, 26, 64; for drink, 58; for entertainment, 58-60

Privy Council, 36, 37, 91, 105, 141

Professional men, in audience, 54, 55, 61

Prostitutes, 75, 92, 96-101

Prynne, William, 6

Puritanism, attitude toward drama, 10, 11, 70

Puttenham, George, 122

Receipts, at Rose Theatre, 26, 27-34, 43, 44, 52, 169-71; for old and new plays, 28, 135

Red Bull Theatre, 65, 88, 90, 122; felony at, 95

Religious scruples, factor in attendance, 68

Renaissance, English, 140

Representative spectator, 155

Restoration theatre, behavior in, 110, 111

Return from Parnassus, The, quoted, 49

Revels Office, 141

Richard II (Shakespeare), 7, 11

Rioting at theatres, 101-8

Romeo and Juliet (Shakespeare), 7

Rose. Theatre, 21, 22, 87; attendance, 20, 30, 33, 34, 36, 44-46; capacity, 29, 34; lord's room, 26n; receipts, 26, 27-34, 43, 44, 52, 171-73, 174-78; seating arrangements, 26

Rowe, John, *Tragi-Comaedia*, quoted, 8-9

Rutland, Earl of, 62, 140

INDEX

St. Paul's Cathedral, walks of, 96, 113

Salisbury Court Theatre, 64

Schelling, Felix E., quoted, 155

Schücking, L. L., 145

Scoloker, Anthony, quoted, 50

Seats, cushioned, 24, 26

Second and Third Blast of Retrait from Plaies and Theaters, A, quoted, 69, 118-19, 174, 175, 176

Shakespeare, William, discontent with audience, 132; imagined as retired from London, 164-65; little experience with private theatres, 87; relation of best works to contemporary drama, 160

plays, appreciated by unintellectual, 134; diverse elements in, 137 ff., 144; drawing power, 35, 47, 48-52; dual meaning in, 145; influenced by audience, 159; theatres used for, 87; a true people's literature, 161

plays, *Hamlet,* 3, 47, 48, 126, 143, 145, 146, 147, 157; *Henry IV,* 7; *Henry VI,* Part I, 48, 136, 176; *Henry VIII,* 87; *King Lear,* 4, 142; *Othello,* 119; *Pericles,* 87; *Richard II,* 7, 11; *Romeo and Juliet,* 7; *Troilus and Cressida,* quoted, 131-32

Shakespeare's audience, *see* Audience, Shakespeare's

Shrove Tuesday riots, 81-82, 107

Sidney, Sir Philip, 140

Sisson, Charles J., 112, 155

Southampton, Earl of, 140

Spanish Tragedy, The (Kyd), 136, 178

Stage-Players Complaint, excerpt, 86

Staple of News, The (Jonson), quoted, 129

Stoll, Elmer E., quoted, 54

Stow, John, 57-58

Strange's Men, 49; receipts of plays produced, 178

Stubbes, Phillip, *The Anatomie of Abuses,* quoted, 97, 106

Suburbs, associated with brothels, 68, 99

Swan Theatre, capacity, 34; description, 21, 22, 25, 45; riot at, 108

Table-books, 120

Tamburlaine (Marlowe), 7, 178

Tarleton, Richard, 110

Taste, unity of, 143-44

Taverns, 57, 95

Taylor, John, 107; *The True Cause of the Water-Mens Suit,* quoted, 36-37

Tewkesbury, 54

Thaler, Alwin, 173

Theatre, The, 21, 22, 35, 57, 87, 103; rocked by earthquake, 106

Theatre, Elizabethan, analogy with motion pictures, 65; danger of emotional appeal in, 118; defended on moral grounds, 72-74; sources of attack on, 11-18

Theatres, accused of enticing workers from work, 14; admission prices, 24, 26, 64; attendance, estimates, 20 ff.; attendance, factors affecting, 65-74; attendance in proportion to population, 41-44; behavior in, 92-116; capacity, 20-23, 29-34; centers of disturbance, 14; chil-